FAN LETTERS

Dear Mr. Trabing,
I just had to let you know how very much I love your writing. You make my day, everyday! You're the "Best in the West."

Dear Wally,
Your column is the one thing in *The Sentinel* that I never fail to read (along with *Peanuts* and *The Far Side*, of course). Please don't be planning to retire. Your column gets better and better; I get the feeling you enjoy writing it.

Dear Wally,
My Mom died at age 93 and she was a save-er of all kinds of things. Out of an almost 50-year-old *Sentinel* newspaper is the reference to something called "caulicab," part cauliflower, part cabbage. We now have a brocciflower. Why? Wasn't it successful? Do you know anything about this? I would love to try this as I really like cabbage, better than broccoli. Could you find out?

Dear Mr. Trabing,
I read your columns from an early age and they were sent to me in care packages in college. I'm sure I owe my 'A's in Expository Writing to you! The professor has certainly appreciated my practiced eye for "the little things" that have formed under your tutelage.

Dear Wally,
Your column today is outstanding. One thoughtful article like that is worth a dozen "clever" ones.

Dear Wally,
I tuned to a radio station. The male speaker quoted a very beautiful and quite nostalgic piece called, "You Lose a Little Bit of Your Child Each Day." It was by someone named Wally Trabing.

Dear Wally,
That Tomato Cake just sounds awful. Would you like my recipe for Mud Pie? I actually have one.

Dear Wally,
You cannot retire!! Won't allow it! I'll protest! Well, you just ruined my day.

Dear Wally,
Thanks for your columns. Like Herb Caen is Mr. San Francisco, you are Mr. Santa Cruz.

THE BEST of Wally Trabing

MOSTLY ABOUT FAMILY

by Wally Trabing

Rising Star Press
Santa Cruz, California

Rising Star Press
Santa Cruz, California
www.RisingStarPress.com

ISBN 0-933670-12-5

Interior and Cover Design by Chuck Spidell, Illusio Design,
www.illusiodesign.com

Copyediting and Additional Interior Production by
Joanne Shwed, Backspace Ink, www.backspaceink.com

Interior Illustrations by Bruce Baillie

Reprint permission granted by *The Santa Cruz Sentinel*, Santa
Cruz, California

Library of Congress Cataloging-in-Publication Data

Trabing, Wally, 1921-
  The best of Wally Trabing : mostly about family / by Wally
Trabing.
        p. cm.
  Summary: "A compilation of humor and perspective
columns by Santa Cruz Sentinel Columnist Wally Trabing.
This volume includes a selection of works that recount family
life in the 1930's through 1960's"–Provided by publisher.
  ISBN 0-933670-12-5 (trade paper : alk. paper)
  I. Title.
  PN4874.T66A25 2004
  814'.6--dc22

                                        2004025414

DEDICATION

This modest tome is rightfully dedicated to my family: my lovely wife, Lois, main supporter since the beginning of time; and my now adult offspring, Mark, graduate of the University of California, Davis; Michael Kent, graduate of Wharton School, University of Pennsylvania; and Mily, graduate of the University of California, Berkeley.

ACKNOWLEDGEMENTS

It is de rigueur that I should acknowledge the *Santa Cruz Sentinel*, breeding place of most of my material that covered humanity at its amusing apex. Also to be acknowledged is its current Publisher Dave Regan who said, "Go for it," and my faithful readers over the decades.

After some 30 satisfying years of column writing for the *Santa Cruz Sentinel* in seaside Santa Cruz, California, and two years as editor of the *UK Eagle* in London, I have shaken off retirement to entertain myself selecting some 100 pieces, some humor, some thoughtfully amusing, and a few introspections for this presentation.

Kids of all ages appear in these columns, making it seem as though I have innumerable offspring. There were only three—written about over a period of years. Mark, Michael Kent, and Mily, and they've promised to forgive me for embarrassing them in print yet one more time.

There is a chapter of memories instilled grandly from living a summer month or so for several years as a towhead kid on a mountain top in a cabin. This was in the start of the 30s when I was still spinning tops. Gramma was settled in the high Pacific coastal hills between Santa Cruz and Watsonville, California, to be near her aging children, scattered in the valleys below. She and I lived out much of the summer like an isolated experiment—lugged-in water, lamp lighted and outhoused—this was Tom Sawyer time.

Just me and Gramma, old but peppy and having fun.

I had to write very well about it because my memory loved it so.

And then there's a chapter concerning my home town of Kingsburg, squeezed in between Thompson seedless grape vineyards, peach orchards, and watermelons in the San Joaquin Valley. Pieces like the one-legged painter with his homemade leg which went crazy in my mother's fashion dress shop! And the time my dignified city attorney father drove our 1925 Maxwell convertible through the rear wall of our garage ending up—well, you'll read where.

Whew!!!

I'll allow you'll find guffaws thither and yon.

TABLE OF CONTENTS

Chapter 1. Mother and the Awful Tower 15

Chapter 2. Kingsburg 23

Nureyev and Me 23

Cussers—Today and Back When 26

Depression Food 28

Memories of a Frantic Family 30

Never on Sunday 33

Songs My Mother Sang...35

The Marvelous Era of "Say Ah" 37

The Way My Father Shaved...39

This Old House: Abandoned But Not Forgotten 42

Those Old Shortcuts 44

The Day Ben Came 46

Chapter 3. Family Life 50

Morning is Our Loveliest Time..50

Dinner Bellows in My Life...53

Bed Making? What's That?...55

A Quiet Game of Cards 58

Clutter in My Life..60

Grand Day About the House 62
Average Busy Family......................................64
Family is Waiting.......................................66
Strange Strain in the Family.........................68
The Halloweening of Uncle Ed.......................70
The Moon is Not My Boon.............................72
Flower Power of the Banjo 74
Don't Put the Car Away!...............................76
Letter From Da Cat.....................................78

Chapter 4. Travels 80
The Trail Talker..80
War and Peace in the Auto...........................82
I Will Get Through, I Will, I Will...................84
Kings Canyon National Park.........................86
Sierra Storm 88
Honey, I Backed Over the Kids.......................90

Chapter 5. Kids...92
Movie Review 92
The Allowance Trauma.................................95
Art of the Big Bandage 97
Teenage Party 99
The Shoe Crisis 101
The Persuading..103
The Stomach Ache.....................................105
Food Detective 107
Making Peace Though Confused 109
Operation Starfish.....................................111
The Manipulator.......................................113
The Bedtime Solution.................................115
Cornflake Kisses Montessori Style 117
Kiss Prints of a Child 119
Lower Lip Power.......................................121
School Inquisitor.......................................123
The Great Potty Sit-Down Strike....................125
The Two-Year-Old Girl................................127
Those Lonely Beginnings 129
War Is a Terrible Thing 132
"Watch!!" 135
Where, Oh Where Has My Little ... .137
The Star of Babble 139
You Lose a Child a Little Every Day...............141
Come Into My Tent!!! 143
The Sniffler 145
Backyard Safari.......................................147

Little Girls' Art of Crying 150
School Buses Are For Catching 152

Chapter 6. Dear Scoutmaster 154
A Memory of Scouting Days 154
Astronomy 156
Cooking—Bromo Seltzer 158
The Hike 160
Dog Care 162
Help! There's a Boa in My Bed! 164
Her Good Turns Are Killing Me 166
The Home Repairer 168

Chapter 7. Man of the House 170
How Supermarkets Make Money 170
I Didn't Get Biscuits 172
The Horse in Me 174
I've Laid a Few Eggs in My Time 176
Midnight Sandwich 178
My Apple Recipe 181
The Bathroom Dilemma 183
Blow the Balloon Wider, Dad! 185
Baby's Birth 187
Don't Honk For My Kid 189
Walter Mitty, Fixit Man 191
Soup on the Wild Side 193
She's Got That Sinking Feeling 195
A Closet Astronaut 197

Chapter 8. Gramma 199
Gramma and the News 199
Ye Olde Outhouse... 204
Gramma's Ears.. 206
Gramma's Storm Magic 208
Tears of My Gramma 211
After Dark Saturday Tub Night.................... 212
Gramma and Mountain Milk 216
Traveling Salesmen...................................... 219
The Saga of Gramma's Pearly Whites.......... 222
Breakfast Call Through the Wall.................. 226
A Little Sundown Music 229
Gramma, The Mountain Banker.................... 231
Gramma and Me as Menders 234
Violent Times with Gramma 237
Gramma vs. the Auto 241
Gramma the Inventor 244
Silences of Gramma...................................... 247

CHAPTER **1**

MOTHER

AND THE AWFUL TOWER

Note: This piece first appeared in the British edition of *Good Housekeeping* in 1951.

For a woman of her age, my mother cut a swath through Europe that would have driven a lesser soul to a rest home. She went everywhere and saw everything with gay abandon and stubborn precision, and neither man, fatigue, nor an interminable series of cathedrals could balk her intention to "do the continent up right"—until she came to the Eiffel Tower.

I'll never forget that anxious week. It took quite a bit out of all our lives. Because of the Tower, Mother overstayed her Paris visit four days and spent every minute of them in a silent battle of pride and healthy fear. And although she conquered in the end and left Paris with her head held high, there was a residue of weariness in her gray eyes that one often observed in combat soldiers after a grueling offensive. Mrs. Dora Watson was partly to blame.

Dora Watson was mother's keen business rival and close friend back home. They both owned and operated ladies' apparel shops in two small neighboring California farming towns.

ing towns. Both were widows over 50; both weighed five pounds more than 195; and both possessed a streak of stubbornness that one seldom found outside a mule.

My wife and I were living in Paris. Like Mother's other projects in life, her coming to Europe was an impulsive phenomenon. One of her weekly letters began: "Dora and I are coming to Paris. Please find us a nice apartment on the Champs Elasy." Except for a few cracks about the Democratic Congress taxing her to death, that was all she said.

Her abruptness was supposed to convey the idea of confidence, but nevertheless, I knew she would be making the trip with many misgivings. She was a fastidiously cautious woman, and at the same time tenacious of a sudden idea. She possessed a cool business head in which there likewise dwelled floating mines of hysteria. Much of her time was spent keeping these traits in balance.

More than anything else, she loved life to run smoothly. Poise, dignity, and sang-froid were, to her, more precious than hope, faith, and charity.

Mother and Dora arrived on the Golden Arrow at the Gare du Nord looking like a couple of Vassar girls. Both wore owlish horn-rimmed glasses with diamond chips peppering the rims, and both were swathed in furs. "Here we are! Here we are!" they cried in the rhythmic tone of a college cheer, as they descended from the Arrow. I was heavily conscious of that fact, as were many other startled arrivers, who could not help but stop and acknowledge it.

In the taxi, on the way to their hotel (who the dickens ever heard of anyone finding an apartment in Paris, let alone on the Champs Elysées?). I was told that their travel agency would take care of everything but their breathing, and except for our regular visits together, there was no reason for me to interrupt my writing schedule.

They held to their word surprisingly well. Once Dora mistook a commuter train for a metro and called me long distance from Chaville to "come fetch" her. Mother howled over this and felt very superior for days until she dropped her glasses in the holy water at Notre Dame. But, except for those minor incidents, their touring flowed smoothly until their last day in Paris when the schedule called for a visit to the Eiffel Tower.

On that afternoon, the telephone rang at my place. It was Dora.

"We're at the Eiffel Tower," she said loudly.

"That's fine," I answered. "You'll get a wonderful view of Paris."

"That's exactly what I said!"

"Well, what's the matter?"

There was a short silence. Then, in a pouty voice, "Your mother won't go up!"

"Why?" I asked, truly surprised.

Dora was slightly deaf, and as we got into the meat of our discourse, her voice grew progressively louder.

"She said she doesn't trust French-made things. ISN'T THAT RIDICULOUS?!!! I TOLD 'ER IT WAS!"

"I should say it is. Tell her there is nothing in the world to worry about. They've been hauling people up and down the Tower for sixty-one years. Tell her that!"

"That's exactly what I told her," confirmed Dora, now yelling, "but your mother just stands there sayin', 'I'd rather be sentenced to hell in a kangaroo court.' She won't even go under it!"

"Well, what can I do?"

"I," screamed Dora defiantly, with a haughty emphasis, "want to go UP!"

When I arrived, they were standing "a safe distance away" like two squatty twins, near the fountains behind the Palais de Chaillot. Mother's face was a tight-lipped blank wall against which Dora still had made no headway.

When Mother saw me approaching, she bristled with added defiance.

"Say what you're going to say, Son, and get it over with. I'm not going up in that awful tower!"

"You're scared," snapped Dora with a curt nod. Her pheasant feather on her straw summer hat followed through.

Mother stiffened and glared at Dora. "You're just as scared as I am, Dora Watson, and you know it. You're just plain stubborn, stubborn. A little breeze and that skinny thing'd crumble like straw!"

"*I'm* stubborn?" crowed Dora, feigning surprise.

Mother sat down on a bench and Dora and I started for the Tower. "You know how I love your mother," said Dora, not ungleefully, "but she's such a fraidy-cat!"

As we crossed the Seine, the Tower loomed up before us and grew higher with each step. Dora hung on to my arm as if we were balancing on a high catwalk.

"I want to go clear to the top!" she said looking back at Mother being stubborn on the bench.

I bought tickets for the troisieme étage, but when the elevator stopped at the first landing, Dora stepped out, pulling me with her. "I think this will be high enough," she said hoarsely. She said it like a sea captain giving an order.

She sat down at one of the little refreshment tables to wait for the return elevator. In the meantime she gave me her green sweater and asked me to go to the railing and wave it down at Mother. "From here, she'll think it's me," said Dora sweetly.

That night when we gathered for our last meal, I thought the Tower incident had been forgotten, but I soon discovered differently. Mother looked like Samson after his haircut, and it didn't take me long to see who the Delilah was.

Through her potage Dora recalled her thoughts in the Eiffel Tower elevator—through the hors-d'oeuvre she extolled the courtesies of the waiter who served her beer on the Eiffel Tower; between bits of ragout she depicted a soul-stirring view from the first landing that I never dreamed existed.

Mother sat silently through the meal, kneading her lips and glaring at Dora. When she tried to change the subject to wonder about the height of a certain monument, Dora used the Eiffel Tower as a yardstick; when Mother asked when the Opera House was built, Dora mused, "Well, let's see, the Tower was constructed in 1889, and ..."

Before the meal was over, Mother had calmed herself and at one point innocently suggested that they should remain in Paris a bit longer. There was no special need to rush on home, "and besides," she said with a peculiar look in her eyes, "I find there are a few things I've forgotten to do." And on the way back to the hotel, when Dora went into a drug store, Mother said to me:

"Will you find time to meet me tomorrow at 2 p.m.?"

"Sure," I said, feeling a little sorry for the browbeating she had taken from Dora. "Where?"

Mother's voice was sharp with self-determination. "Under the Eiffel Tower," she said.

We met coming out of the Trocadero metro station the next afternoon and started toward the Tower—Mother marvelously fighting a desire to collapse.

"I didn't feel well at all yesterday," she said with forced naturalness. Then she got to the point. "Dora's been acting as if she scaled Lord Nelson's monument!"

In the elevator, Mother immediately fastened herself around the white center pole with one arm, gripped me with the other, and with a painful effort said, "I wish to visit the second floor."

"Okay," I said, "but open your eyes so you can see the view."

The elevator came to life with an elastic bounce and set-tled down to a slanting climb up one of the steel-grated pant legs of the Tower. Other tourists in the car, chatter-ing excitedly in several different languages, gave Mother a trifle more confidence, and she looked around for someone to whom to show it off. Her victim was the hollow-eyed French conductor, dreamily enjoying his between-floor stu-por. He was slumped almost up to his stained moustache in a drab, blue uniform, near the center pole.

"It's nice," said Mother suddenly and loudly.

The way she said it sounded like "*Help*!" in any language, and the little man whirled around, wide-eyed and startled.

"It's nice." She almost yelled it. Mother was under the impression that if one spoke English loud enough to the French, they would somehow be forced to understand. The conductor gave Mother the pleasant but idiotic grin he re-served for tourists who became familiar.

"He didn't understand," Mother guessed, and was vexed.

"He doesn't understand English, Mother," I said.

"Oh, dear, he thinks I'm ridiculous—you'd better explain to him!"

I told the conductor that my mother thought it was very nice.

"Comment?" drawled the man, obviously wishing the whole affair could be dropped.

I repeated that my mother thought the Tour Eiffel was nice. Mother over-smiled and made wide sweeping gesticulations with her hands.

The old man resigned his eyes towards Mother and wagged his head (rather violently, I thought) in affirmation, but I could easily see that he hated every blessed bolt and girder of the thing.

I bought more tickets on the first landing and we went on up to the second. When we arrived, Mother refused to go within 30 feet of the parapet, but stood near the elevator entrance and clung to a steel support.

"Mother," I called from the railing, "come and see the view!"

"Yes, isn't it magnificent," she called weakly. "Let's go down!"

That night we had a dinner speaker. It was Mother.

"Dora, you wouldn't know what a magnificent city Paris is if you haven't seen it from the duuzeem floor. We stopped at the first floor and I couldn't see a thing." (That was because Mother had her eyes closed.) "It's a pity you didn't go to the second landing. Really, Dora, there was nothing to it!"

Dora played with her soup like one searching for fish bones. Her pout gave her face a Ubangi look. When she managed to get a word in to wonder how far it was to Versailles, Mother chirped sweetly, "I believe it's twenty kilometers from the Eiffel Tower."

The next afternoon, Dora went clear to the top, and the ticket lady and I began a nodding acquaintance.

Faust, that evening, was brilliantly performed as usual. Mephisto was splendid in his crafty intrigue with the old doctor, and Marguerite's plight gave the opera a tinge of old-fashioned melodrama. Mother and Dora missed the presentation. They were in attendance, but they spent most of the five acts glaring at each other.

Dora never once mentioned the Tower, but that was hardly necessary. She sat huffed in her upholstered box seat and gave a reading with her eyes.

"One could stand on a milk-stool and get a view equal to that from the second landing. *I* went to the top! *I* went to the top. *I* went to the top!" Marguerite went to heaven and Mephisto went back to hell.

"Deaux Billets au troisieme étage," I said to the woman in the Eiffel Tower ticket booth. She looked at me as if she wanted to ask a question, but at the last second, restrained herself.

As the elevator began its long climb, Mother's face was transfixed with the expression of one rising to meet his Maker, not quite sure that he would make it through the Holy Customs on the way.

At the top we stepped out on to the open platform into a stiff, buffy wind that whistled through the criss-cross wires of the railing. Mother's face was as white as the dome on Sacré Coeur and she clung to my arm as if it were life itself.

We walked to the railing which came flush with Mother's nose.

Dora had mentioned casually that she had dared to look over and down, and Mother had reluctantly caught the challenge.

Inch by inch she slid her nose over, clutching me tighter to her bosom as she did so. When it reached the outer edge, she rolled her bulging eyes groundward. Paris spread out beneath and beyond, like a great semicircle garden of gray and green. In the distance it blended its grays with a foggy mist that evanesced into a rich blanket of blue.

"There's the Arc de Triomphe," said Mother, finally finding part of her voice. She pointed with her eyes. And, as the significance of the grand panorama before her made itself felt, Mother gradually relaxed. Her eyes were slowly filling with that glint of exhilaration mountain climbers show upon reaching a virgin peak. I could see that she still felt about as secure as a fly trying to hang upside down on ice and that her instincts urged her to get down off the awful tower, and back on that bench near the Trocadero. But there was something more deeply embedded inside Mother that had won. It was an awful stubborn something that had pride to it.

"Well, I made it," she said, slightly pushing out her chin and looking about her, as if in search of Dora.

"See, it wasn't so bad," I said, smiling.

"Was Dora scared?"

I was rather proud. "Scareder than you," I said.

A certain peace of mind reflected across her face as my words sunk in. In fact, as we stood there on the platform I saw in her face a new brazen fearlessness that I hardly expected Mother to display. It seemed to envelop her in spite of herself.

Suddenly her lips compressed slightly, and with a supercilious air, her eyes traveled measuringly up the thin steel ladder that led to the tiny weather station perched 40 feet above the platform.

"Mother," I said firmly, "I think we had better go down!"

~

CHAPTER **2**

KINGSBURG

NUREYEV AND ME

When Rudolf Nureyev was at his peak in ballet, I would lapse into a trance of pleasure following his graceful movements. It brought back to me my hallowed day as a dancer. At my height, I was a carrot in the second grade spectacular presentation, *Mr. Gregory's Cabbage Patch*.

I am not so naive as to assume any of you might remember my performance.

Everyone (except my mother) called it a catastrophe. It had its opening (and closing) on an Off-Broadway stage in an elementary school in Kingsburg, California.

Even today I am approached by sensitive personages who notice my theatrical bent, and I have to confess my carrot performance. While it did not rate seven curtain calls, it was a highlight in my young career.

We in the cast were not allowed to stay up for the review. Our town paper did not come out until three days after the spectacular.

I was chosen as a carrot mainly because, at this physiological stage in my life, I LOOKED like a carrot. I wanted to be a turnip, but the carrot cardboard cutout was tall, skinny, and tapered, and I was the only member of the class who would fit behind it.

The reason I made only one appearance was that Flora (the tomato) ripped part of my carrot because she claimed that I bumped her off the stage.

That was balderdash!

I was supposed to hop over to the tomato to demonstrate a crush on her. In doing so, I innocently overhopped. It drew small applause.

She was built somewhat in the shape of her tomato, so she squished softly when she landed offstage.

Our drama teacher was a tall austere woman with a terra-cotta complexion and a slightly migraine smile, who assumed that there was a spark of Nijinsky or Pavlova in all of us!

Although most of us were more physically suited to portray Don Knotts.

There was another reason I left the stage at the height of my glory.

I was a practical lad, given to reading *Jane Eyre* and pamphlets on egg production, and I think I sensed—and time has proven me right—that there would never be an overwhelming demand for carrots in ballet.

The show was a benefit to raise money for a stage curtain.

There was no curtain at the time, and we all appeared on stage via the clever procedure of requesting that the audience close its eyes and then, on the command of "Open," there we were!

The PTA was hoping to turn the proceeds over to the curtain committee, but it was overruled. The vegetables committee (the esteemed actors) leaned toward "blowing the dough" on ice cream.

At one point during the play, my role called for me to run across the stage, "sur les points," chased by a cannibalistic bunny rabbit who had designs on my person.

The action took place at sundown which required that the janitor slowly pull the shades down in the room.

On stage, the rabbit was up to no good, it loved yummy vegetables, especially carrots, and was headed toward me!

Well, it so happened that I had buddies among the giant squash and watermelon and they moved about to block the bad rabbit's path!

Later one disgruntled man in the audience said the effect was more like *The Rape of the Sabines*!!

To be truthful, I've been told by those who have memories of elephants that my fame was established by a frantic, grand leap known in old Germany as "un snozboomer"!!!

It almost wiped out the entire vegetable cast.

I was so dazed, it allowed the rabbit to catch me two scenes before he was supposed to, and he ate me, ending the show.

Our drama teacher came out, giving me a migraine smile, and asked the audience to close its collective eyes.

On my way out, I was tripped by the onion!!

He had a crush on the tomato.

The principal, apparently so impressed with the show, commented to one of the teachers that the cast should go on the stage. He winked and cracked, "The first one out of town."

~

I guess it has been many a year since a kid has tasted soap because of a spicy tongue.

It used to be one of the great enemies of profanity.

Only then, we called it cussin'.

I had one of the cleaner mouths in Kingsburg during my marble-playing days because my mother was always washing it out with soap.

Lemon, I think it was.

"What did you say, young man?"

"Nothin'."

"I heard you!"

Lady parents did not spank as a rule; that was the male department.

"All I said was damnation, like Grandpa always says."

"The Lord will punish you," my mother would say, but the Lord never moved fast enough for her.

I was led to the bathroom by the ear, my lips compressed, but not compressed enough.

Soap is slippery and easy to administer.

She would force it in and then let me go to swish water and grape juice around my mouth.

I learned not to clench my teeth during these occasions for the soap would cling to them. It was harder to get off and the taste was awful.

Colorful cussing is an art involving timing and selective expletives not used by the common herd.

Those were tamer times in Kingsburg, but not tame enough for mothers. I think they thought cussing originated in the mouth.

Anyway, that is where they applied the curative.

To this day I don't like lemon soap.

Ivory soap came in block form and wasn't used for discipline, for it was difficult to apply to a boy's small mouth.

Today's soaps are filled with perfumes and all sorts of pleasantries.

It probably tastes better, too, and therefore not as effective as a cussing deterrent.

Besides, I don't think there is enough soap around to correct the current blue atmosphere.

My mother, in her mini-lectures, used to say that swearing was a sign of an inferiority complex. It showed a lack of ability to express oneself.

I'd pick up a new word or two around the raisin packing sheds, from the hoboes coming through town, or from Steinbeck's *Grapes of Wrath* which I found along the highway.

I got a double soaping for an "SOB." My "damnations" came from my grandfather, whom I liked to copy. I even tried to spit tobaccy like him, but failed.

Kingsburg was not a swearing town. Oh, you'd hear "by yimminy" or "yumpin Jehoshaphats," but in general, it was a gentle town filled with gentle people.

As a parent, I never got around to using soap on my young cussers.

Soap nowadays is filled with vitamins and I don't want healthier cussers!

~

By the tail end of the Depression, I was old enough to remember the effect it had on our meals. We managed well enough, but there were norm differences.

My father had developed an affinity for horseradish and pickled pigs' feet and this put him in a special category.

In the first place it was "foreign food" in our San Joaquin Valley town. He used horseradish like kids today use catsup.

On occasions when we used candles at the table we begged him to light them.

For my mother used to say, "Don't strike a match too near your father. He'll breathe fire like a dragon."

The pickled pigs' feet jar was always in the ice box and on the table at meal times.

In those days it was a cheap delicacy and no one else in the family could stomach them. It was his private property by default.

Jackrabbits were another common food.

They roamed the miles of vineyards around Kingsburg by the thousands. We weren't hunters but they would be brought to us skinned and ready for the skillet.

My father was an attorney and during the Depression years it was not unusual for farmers to pay my father for legal services with food. We ate well. He kept a big ledger in his law office, peppered with such entries as:

"Jess Swanson, family will, two turkeys."

"Aldo Johnson, property damage suit, first payment, cured ham and two boxes of Thompson seedless grapes."

"Mrs. Betty Betts, appearance, traffic court, six jars strawberry preserves."

It got so that we built a small coop behind the garage to keep the extra fowl until time came to eat them.

Rabbits were plentiful; there were lugs of ripe peaches, clothed in swirls of rich redness, pregnant with juice. They were stored in the big back porch pantry until my mother could get the Mason jars sterilized and the wax melted.

There was no refrigeration then; fruit had to be dealt with while the natural freshness was intact.

In the 100-degree afternoons, I could faintly see my mother behind clouds of steam, tonging the gleaming fruit into jars.

Watermelons, so big they were not practical to put on the market bins, were wrestled into a backyard bin, sometimes three feet long and so filled with sweet ripeness they would burst with a rippling explosion merely by breaking the rind with a fork.

The payoff in eggs was very popular. My father never charged large fees and the farmers appreciated this by bringing in quality food. We had angel-food cake more than most people because my mother had to use up the eggs, and it took a lot to bake the cake.

Those cakes were so light she had to put a frying pan on top when it came from the oven, so as to keep it from floating away.

Those were the days, my friends. A few Swedes would bring lutefisk, dried cod from the old country. I mean you could use it as a baseball bat. It took a week to soften, soaked in a kind of lye and a flavor that made sawdust taste like candy.

Yes, those were the days.

~

If it were not for a nature film I once saw in which the narrator claimed that ants running wildly about on top of a disturbed ant hill were, in fact, a superbly organized family reacting to a pre-set plan, I would be a haggard human wreck by now.

Looking back I see a similarity.

The family of my youth was fraught with such emergencies. We displayed a frantic looseness that was startling. But we held together.

Such occasions were told and retold in family gatherings.

Such as the time my father drove his new Model T touring car forward clean through our garage wall while attempting to back out.

The car wiped out a clothesline of Monday wash on the other side.

As my father sat ghost-like under freshly drying sheets and a scattering of my mother's bras, my mother rushed out and fell into her bed of prize carnations, sputtering, "CHARLIE, YOU FOOL, LOOK WHAT YOU DID TO MY CARNATIONS!!!"

She always entered her carnations in the Fresno County Fair.

Mother fell down quite often, actually.

Her legs were slightly bowed and did not operate well at certain speeds.

Mother also fell down in the front yard. She had loaned money to the local lumberyard that burned down quite regularly.

When the fire siren wailed on top of the Kingsburg water tower, she would rush from the house sniffing and searching the skyline for smoke.

Our sidewalk took a sharp left angle to turn to the street, and often she failed to make the turn and fell into a flower bed of mums and baby's breath.

My job was to answer her shrieks with a bottle of smelling salts and try to find her head somewhere among the flora.

Now, this is not to say that Mother was scatterbrained.

Nay. It was just that within her placid mind there dwelled pockets of hysteria.

A good example of this was the night "the roof fell in."

The roof did not actually fall in, which always confuses people when the story is told.

What happened was simply that their bed boards gave out in the middle of the night.

And my father, who had a great fear of earthquakes, yelled out, "WE'VE HAD IT!!"

My mother, groggy with sleep, misinterpreted this as, "YOU'VE HAD IT!"

And, assuming that my father had suddenly gone mad, and was about to do her in, she whapped him in the face with her hot water bottle.

Which was under her pillow due to an earache.

It was not unreasonable for my father to believe that the roof HAD fallen in and this is why the incident is referred to as the night the roof fell in, instead of the time the bed broke down.

It was peacefully resolved and by the time we kids crowded into the bedroom to catch the action, they were in each other's arms. We emitted a symphony of giggles that would challenge a Looney cartoon.

But, getting to our immediate family's panics, I soon discovered I had inherited my father's sense of, as they were called, "night frights." When the kids were young and would scream in the night or one of Santa Cruz's earthshakes occurred, I would react like a fireman whose boots had been borrowed by an off-duty buddy for a clam dig.

I would dash blindly into the closet and fall among an octopus of wire coat hangers. The family would have to get up and "dig" me out.

It is said, with a rash of knee-slapping and eye-rolling, that I caused more emergencies than there were emergencies.

But we have a way of rallying to off-beat causes.

An emergency of a lesser nature might illustrate this.

Being long of legs, when I am struck with a Charley horse cramp I will confess to anything if it will bring relief.

Long ago I organized an emergency scheme to handle the problem.

When this dreaded cramp came on I yelled out "CHARLEY HORSE!"

This was the signal for whoever was nearby to rush in and jump on my knee or knees to straighten out my leg or legs.

I have had as many as three persons sitting on my leg or legs at one time, a sight that would likely raise questions as to the family's mental health should it be known.

We merely called it Emergency Plan 22-C.

~

I can't remember where the idea started or what the reason behind it was, but when I was a kid in Kingsburg, we never went "out front" on Sunday.

"You kids get in the backyard! Don't you know what day it is?"

If this occurred today, we would have said, "Yeah, so it's Sunday. What difference is there in observing the Lord's Day whether we're in the front yard or backyard?"

If I had said this then, questioning my Dad's rods, he would have gotten directly to the seat of the issue—my seat!

He would have roared with laughter over the crop of fish-spined parents of today, then roared with scorn. He was a roarer.

Kingsburg on Sundays resembled a funeral parlor—between funerals. Poke your nose inside one some time if you can't imagine what it is like.

The reason was probably lost in antiquity. It mattered little. I think it was a discipline, and I think it made us freer than kids are today—freer inside.

There was nothing open on Sunday—except one rebel cigar store (there was only one) where the evil clicking of pool balls could be heard as we walked quickly by.

Not that we ever got downtown much on Sunday.

We could climb trees in the back, but we couldn't yell from the top branches the way we could on Saturdays.

The town came alive only briefly on Sunday and this was during church services.

Church bells blended in competitive harmony, reaching deep into the fruit-jungled country where most of the people lived.

We used to brag that Kingsburg had more churches per capita than any town in the country.

What made it appear spectacular, of course, was that the town was sort of an open space between a great ocean of Thompson seedless vineyards and orchards. Still is.

In the fresh earliness of a hot Sunday morning the town would be empty, then, like crowds gathering from off-stage in a giant musical, people came. Everyone in their Sunday uniforms—suits and fine dresses that had not left the closet since the Sunday before.

And then the town would be strangely empty again as worshippers disappeared into their veneered holiness until they spilled out after church in mingling confusion, slowly sorting themselves out into homebound units.

The town was a unit in those days. We knew what was expected of us, if not by law, then by tradition and experience.

So we played in the backyard. So it might have been hypocritical.

But, those were free days. By 2 p.m., anyone driving down Draper Street had to be an out-of-towner.

Some of whom thought, "I like the peacefulness here—think I'll settle."

~

My mother, at 83, drove up from Kingsburg last week, managing to do so without acquiring a speeding ticket, and brought with her some old songs she used to sing.

She is getting sentimental in her "middle years," as she puts it, and wanted to divide her sheet music between my brother and me.

She used to sing at funerals, for the church and occasionally in the park on Saturday night with the Kingsburg Home Town Concert Band.

I remember those hot summer valley nights when the band would finish some thundering march like *Under The Double Eagle*, and then she would walk out in a large picture hat, into the glaring lights and the band would ooze into *Peg O' My Heart*, or *Marchet* and her voice would fan out from the smooth band shell under the city water tank and into the hot night where we blanket-sat on the grass.

And my brother, wrestling over by the water fountain, would "give up," "shush" the gang and say, "That's my ma up there!"

I also remember that the sheet music was kept in the piano bench along with crumbs from spent cookies, hidden there to break up our forced hour at the piano.

There was always a lot of trillin' and scale singing around that piano.

I hold a vague image of her practicing for a funeral—my mother and another woman in duet, dolefully wrenching out *A Perfect Day* or *One Fleeting Hour*, with a male accompanist who had fuzzy hair, a ramrod back and whose hands made constant high jumps in slow motion over the keys.

And I remember my father grumbling in the kitchen, "My God, they've got a funeral going out there without a body!"

At the Tuesday Club she would render *I Bring You Lilies From My Garden* or thrill the ladies with *I Love a Little Cottage*.

The sheet music she brought is dull-colored with age; the more popular songs are slightly tattered from long handling in nervous hands.

"Yeah, Yeah," was not even a gleam in the songwriter's father's eye.

Lyrics dealt with heaven, faded roses, endless nights, bitter tears, 'neath the stars, sweethearts, and dreams that did or didn't come true.

On the back of *When I Lost You*, by Irving Berlin, he plugs another song, saying, "This song surpasses all my previous efforts. I can safely say this is the best song I ever wrote." This was 1914.

The song is *Along Came Ruth*. Never heard of it.

I note that *I'm Sorry I Made You Cry*, by N. J. Clesi, "is also to be had for your Talking Machine or Player Piano."

I don't know what I'm going to do with all these songs. *Good Night, Little Girl, Good Night* or *Oh Promise Me* are lousy on the banjo.

But they are family relics and thus among things to be kept.

Who knows, *Be My Little Baby Bumble Bee* may make a comeback.

If it does, I'll be ready.

~

THE MARVELOUS ERA OF "SAY AH"

I grew up in the miracle era of medicine when most deep-seated ailments could be cured by removing the tonsils.

No matter where the pain was, your mother would bring you to the doctor's office where you would automatically open your mother and say, "ah."

The doctor did not speak regular English. He had his own language.

"Ah, ah-ha, mmmmmmm, wider, uh-huh!"

Then he would take your mother aside near his wall of medical books and, in a low voice, say, "Tonsils."

While you sat in the chair with your mouth still half-open, wondering why it's taking them so long to plan a funeral.

It had its drawbacks. Once the tonsils were removed the doc was limited in his diagnosis.

It also was a great era for wound closing.

They used more tape then to close cuts and as a result we have better scars than the kids of today.

I can show you some 40-year-old scars today that still rate sympathy and "tsk tsk."

Appendix scars were works of art—more like a weld than a suture. As I remember, it was quite daring for a girl to show her scar. As I remember, it was usually on a dare.

Most kids today wouldn't know an enema bag if they saw one.

I can still see it hanging in the bathroom like a threat.

The sight of it kept us hearty.

Another great preventive medicine was castor oil.

We took it for both physical and moral ailments. The administration of it depended upon the occasion. When it was given for cussing my father wouldn't hold our noses.

My mother kept it in plain sight in the same cupboard as the sweets. It cut down overindulgence.

She also had faith in bread and milk poultice and mustard plaster, spread out over the chest like a sandwich gone mad and we would lie there dripping, wondering about her sanity.

There was a great deal of feet soaking, too.

People don't seem to soak their feet anymore. This was the era of Epsom salts.

It was the nickname we used for our grammar school nurse. She had us do everything but smoke it when we complained.

But, during the winter, we soaked our feet a lot at home. It also washed them, which I think was the primary purpose.

Over all, the main medicine in those Kingsburg days was called "attitude."

We were not supposed to cuss or get too fresh with the girls, or lie or steal, or get sick.

When the first rains began, my mother would say, "Now, we are not going to have any colds this winter."

She said it in her disciplinary voice.

Also, bleeding was not tolerated unless we had a good flow going.

Of course, we were urchins of the soil and it took some ambitious bleeding to show through the dirt.

We had it another way over today's kids.

We didn't need vitamins. We ate food before it got into the hands of the processors.

And if we did get sick we were put to bed. It speeded the "recovery."

If we were well enough to get up we were well enough to do work around the house or go to school. This left bed or responsibility.

A very healthy check and balance system which took the fun out of being sick.

~

Shaving is so easy and effortless today (twist, click, buzz) that sometimes I feel downright silly moving that purring machine around my face.

Especially when I have such a clear mental picture of the routine my father went through each morning.

It was a man's job, then.

It took a virile spirit to power that long, straight-edge razor around the throat and up the cheek.

The scraping of it against his face would pull me awake of a morning—in the next room.

This was in Kingsburg where we lived in a brown house and could see the snow cap of the Sierra in the distance, through the San Joaquin Valley heat curtain.

Those were the days of the bathroom hot water heater that hung above the tub and roared like a ship's boiler and when you lighted it, the flames spiraled up around the water tank and it sounded like a rocket launching.

I never got to light it until I was 15.

My father got "firsts" in the bathroom.

I grew into teenhood seeing him framed by the bathroom door in his blue suit pants and Long John underwear that covered him to his wrists, and his light gray suspenders that hung down behind.

He was raised on a Wyoming sheep ranch near Medicine Bow and his skin was tough from the cold winters there.

I remember his face: big, with large pores that manufactured tough, bristly whiskers, pleading for a chance to show their stuff.

But he was the town's judge and had to look stern and smooth.

He would soak a small towel until wisps of steam came from its hotness.

This he slapped around his face until only the tip of his nose showed through. When he misjudged the heat, there would be muffled words under the towel that were not in my vocabulary then.

For the lathering, he had a white mug. There was a rose painted on one side and the word "Charlie" underneath, in a fancy scroll.

That was his first name—"Charlie."

And I remember his flared-out, stubby brush with a rather classy ivory handle and a round cake of soap in the bottom of the mug and the "clok, clok, clok, clok" that came from working up a lather as the brush knocked against the sides.

The sound was as regular as the chimes from the old clock in the living room or the Southern Pacific Midnight Owl passenger train that raced through Kingsburg as if chased by ghosts or my mother's peculiar call that breakfast was ready.

It made a beautiful lather, like whipped cream on dessert, and my father would apply it to his face with a special flourish—when he was happy.

The straight-edge razor was a blade to respect.

It was off limits to the kids.

Under no circumstances were we ever to touch it, so, of course, we did, and got clean, bloody cuts for our curiosity.

We hid the blood like secret treasure and kept the cut finger folded during meals.

My father kept the razor honed and the sound was always with us.

The razor strop was a permanent fixture next to the bathroom sink.

His was made of fine leather with a strap backing that cracked when we were spanked with it.

But of a morning he would run his razor up and down the strop with fine, even strokes, his face white with frothy soap—up and down, up and down, turning the razor with a quick flip of the wrist.

When shaving, he held it just so in his right hand, with the little finger sticking out as if in a gesture of finesse.

He started near his Adam's apple and worked upward, his great chin thrust outward.

When shaving his upper lip, his eyes would close and then for the down stroke at the temple, his face would take on an angelic blissfulness, and he would make an "O" with his mouth when the strokes came to the lower cheeks.

At the chin, he would make a horrendous face, and while scraping just under it, his mouth would clamp and bunch like Popeye's.

When he was through, the blade would be folded back into the fancy ivory handle, and then he would pat his jowls with a fresh smelling aftershave.

The men in Kingsburg had clean shaves in those days.

I don't remember him making many "gotcha" slips.

Which was amazing, for the straight-edge was unforgiving.

It was not of the sissified ilk we used today. No "clicks" or protective covers.

But, no, if you're thinking what I think you are, I don't want to go back. I'll stick with my electric, thank you.

~

Seldom are abandoned houses allowed to die a natural death, like they did when I was playing mumblety-peg.

I knew one that stood waiting on the edge of my home town of Kingsburg, hidden among the vineyards of the San Joaquin Valley.

The edge of town was never far from the center, for in the heart of this great valley fruit bowl, productive land gave in grudgingly to asphalt.

The old house was non-Victorian and eyeless, with no glass left to reflect the season.

There was no front door to state its preference of guests or its demand for privacy or feeling of welcome.

It stood alone against a border of vineyards next to a crippled windmill with no rudder to guide the panels into the breeze.

The yard was overgrown with high weeds as in an unkempt grave, packaged from neater surroundings by a rickety picket fence.

There must be a house like this in most memories over 40.

The old place in my past clung to the land, gradually adopting its color, texture, and odor.

Dark mossy shingles curled upward at the ends like freed toes, and the front porch sagged comfortably toward the cracked sidewalk which ran through a corridor of a brown lawn gone wild.

On a free day, when mischief needed release, we would wander from room to room, testing echoes, inventing legends and half wishing-up daylight ghosts.

Or at least a sleeping hobo from the nearby Southern Pacific tracks.

The urge to destroy and deface was not a sociological need back then.

Rather we used the abandoned hulk to feed our minds with melancholy and search for clues to its homier past.

We found them always.

Browned pine needles in a rug-less corner told of Christmases past, when shouts of joy filled the room.

Someone, long into dust, had preferred flowering relief moldings rather than plain.

Lighter rectangular spots on the faded wallpaper told of seascapes or portraits that once hung there.

A small, awkwardly drawn doll in crayon on a wall told us of a mischievous child and a scolding mother.

In a bedroom, a doll's arm in an empty, broken dresser drawer lined with an ancient *Fresno Bee* told us of a mother's tidiness and a child's presence.

The musty mysteriousness never left us.

Gossamer curtains as delicate as burned gas mantles collapsed at a touch, and in the bathtub there were skeletons of mice with tiny, grinning skulls. Past tragedies.

Their fate drew our shudders as did the sudden flight of a disturbed bat from a darkened corner.

I remember the narrow stairways that led to eerie, dimly lit upper rooms, their windows blindfolded by weathered boards.

We feared the climb, though we'd been there many times.

Each stair step played its own tuneless warning and we would cluster, combining our bravery by holding hands as we neared the top.

Surviving murder and mayhem, we would celebrate the letdown by jumping from closets screaming "BOO!!" and when that wore ineffective, we peeked through boarded windows to view the vast stretch of Thompson seedless vineyards that melted into the Sierra to the east.

Occasionally the wind would catch a vane of the windmill and it would make a screeching, half-hearted attempt to spring to life—but never did.

Only a grand wisteria vine that snaked new feelers along the ridge of the roof remained in residence.

The old house was its only companion and it clung to it with an impressive love.

Eventually, the old place went, though. The last time I was there, it was gone; my monument to the past is no more.

May it rest in peace.

~

THOSE OLD SHORTCUTS

Whenever I spot a scar of white dirt angling across a corner vacant lot through tall spring weeds, I have a yearning to take off my shoes and give it a walk.

This would look foolish, wouldn't it?

I mean, I would have to explain to anyone peering on that I subscribed to the *Saturday Review* and gave to United Fund and am not at this time planning to overthrow the government.

So I pass on the urge, maybe looking back once or twice as I pass by.

They're rather rare sights these days—shortcuts.

Mostly swallowed up by houses now or corralled by fences or placed off limits by the pinch-nosed pride of ownership.

Kingsburg was a shortcut kind of town when I was still being told to be seen, not heard.

They were fixtures. It was as if certain lots had been set aside by nature for this purpose.

Some of the old lots are still there today.

You might even call them landmarks if you look back through the eyes of a small boy.

In the winter the dirt paths were fainter, blending in with the frost-covered stubble.

But in the summer they divided the tall weeds like a winding river from the air.

Some were worn ankle deep into the soft, sandy San Joaquin Valley earth that has furnished the nation with fruit and produce for generations.

They were our roads, for a kid wouldn't think of "going around" when he could "cut across."

I don't remember ever going by road to our swimming hole in the irrigation ditch that slashed through the sea of Thompson seedless vineyards behind the Satterburg ranch.

We would cut through the old Bonesteel place, turn left at the chicken sheds and then angle south a bit to miss the Ben Hanson house, cross four or five lots to the edge of the vineyards, and then take the path which stair-stepped from one straight vine-lined row after another, slanting toward the "drop" where we gathered to swim.

The nature of the shortcut, of course, is to reduce effort.

This is why, when a tree fell across an old established shortcut, one could see the consternation written on the ground.

Some figured a certain way around the tree was shorter to regain the old path; others went another route until finally some kind of a collective decision would be reached, which would ultimately show in the stronger path.

The other would become fainter as the followers acceded to the majority until it became only a suggestion to wonder about, like an ancient Indian trail.

Even our dogs, which I don't suppose cared one way or another which way they went, took our shortcuts when they wandered out alone. From the habit of following us, I guess.

Sometimes, as an adult, I think too much cement and paved ways have led to some of our plastic views of life.

We ought to go back over some of the old paths and get the feel of the earth again.

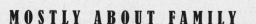

Whenever I smell paint or see a wooden leg, or hear women screaming, the name of Ben Skagaway comes rushing back to my mind.

Ben painted one room of my mother's home every year, and he was a thorough worker, a quality my mother admired. But on the debit side he had two marks.

He drank. Secondly, he had a wooden leg.

Mr. Skagaway lost his leg at the hip in a railroad accident and made his own replacement in his workshop.

Those privileged to see it told their friends, who told others, that it was of good quality pine and literally encased within were long springs, short springs, levers, latches, pulleys, catches, hinges, and straps.

From a distance his bearing was true and his gait smooth. But up close, each step sounded like a screen door opening, and sometimes the hinges squeaked.

Before coming to paint, he made it a practice to drop by and look over the job. My mother, whose nerves I'm convinced were frayed from birth, would leave carefully written instructions for me or my brother to hand to Ben Skagaway, for she refused to be in the same room with him when he sat down.

When Mr. Skagaway sat down, he would cross his wooden leg over his good knee and force it down with his hand. He held it down with noticeable effort, in somewhat the manner of one setting a rat trap, until he adjusted the latch which would lock it in place.

But through the years my mother was to learn that this latch was by no means reliable.

Often as not, during a lull in the conversation, the latch would give away and the powerful springs would explode his leg straight again with a quivering "TWAAAANNNNGGG!!!"

I think my mother would rather lose blood than dignity, but on these occasions she would let out a wild scream that would frighten Mr. Skagaway half to death. So it was silently and mutually agreed to work through written instructions.

And as I mentioned, Mr. Skagaway drank, which led to the day he came to tell my mother he couldn't paint the house—mainly because he couldn't see it too well.

My mother owned a ladies apparel store next to our house and ran it with a sedate hauteur that won her the more uppity class of customer in Kingsburg.

When my brother or I had to enter the back room on an errand, we had to walk stooped so as not to startle the half-dressed ladies. We tried to reason with her that her ladies would be more likely to stampede at the sight of a male sneaking around in a crouched position than a male upright, but the rule remained to "stoop."

I remember it was midmorning, and I was well along covering the furniture and preparing the room for the painter.

I had rigged up a cow bell in the kitchen with a cord to the store and suddenly it rang so violently it came off its hook and bellowed to the floor, and I got to the kitchen in time to see the cord disappearing in short frantic jerks.

I ran into the back of the store in my usual stooped position, but what I saw over the counter straightened me up fast.

At first, it appeared that my mother and Ben Skagaway were Indian wrestling on the display room floor. Both were making little incoherent noises and the customers had fled screaming to the small dressing rooms lining the wall.

What had happened was he had come to the front door to tell my mother he could not paint. On hindsight, the whole affair could have been settled with three or four perfunctory words; but my mother tried to whisper for him to "go away" from a distance too far for him to hear, and when he tried to close the range, he tripped and fell on the door sill.

It is still debated in our family whether my mother fainted in Mr. Skagaway's direction or whether she deliberately tried to break his fall.

At any rate, the two met at roughly a 45-degree angle and, like a tent without its middle pole, sagged slowly to the floor.

I lifted my mother to her feet and then tried to lift Mr. Skagaway. But as I did, a strange thing occurred. He began to grow longer.

My mother, wisps of gray hair half hiding her face, stared with unbelieving eyes.

"Dear God!" she cried hoarsely, "the man's coming apart."

This information carried an appalling impact to the ladies hidden in the dressing rooms. Someone screeched.

The explanation was simple. Mr. Skagaway's wooden leg straps had broken in his fall. It lay naked on the floor, bent in a semi-squatting position; the long screen-door springs quivering like tired muscles.

Mother, a short, squarish woman, backed away slowly, eyeing the leg with owlish suspicion. She could have been more easily persuaded to shake hands with a corpse than touch the painter's anatomic woodwork, so I leaned Mr. Skagaway against a dress rack and picked up the leg.

My mother was pressed against the counter hissing, "Don't stand like a fool, get him out!"

The painter was not with us. His eyes looked like oil-soaked agates and his smile held a blissful vacancy.

I was doing my best to analyze the maze of springs and gadgets in order to straighten out the leg when my mother decided to act. It made her mad when Mr. Skagaway began to sing, so she strode forward and grabbed the leg. One of us must have tripped the right catch, for the leg sprang into life with a steely snap and leaped into the air.

On her third try, mother screamed and started to run. The effect was atomic to the ladies in the booths who could not see what was happening. But all in all I think my mother got the worst of it.

When the leg hit the floor, instead of staying there, it bounded up again and, as if possessed with a misogynous soul, veered in her direction.

She took three measured steps and hurdled the jewelry counter and fell like a seasoned pole-vaulter amid a pile of cardboard hat boxes, where she lay making little cooing noises through her nose.

It's difficult to put into words the conglomeration of sounds from all parties at this moment. About the closest I can come is the long-playing version of Stravinsky's *Fire Bird Suite* played at 78 rpm.

I dragged Mr. Skagaway out the back door, laid him on the lawn, and placed his versatile leg under his head. When I went back in the shop, the ladies were standing in a tight circle awaiting a turn at the smelling salts.

No one was laughing and mother looked tired and changed.

However, she was never a person to hold a grudge, so Mr. Skagaway was allowed to return the next day and paint the room. He returned each year until he died.

I think out of appreciation Ben got the latch on his wooden leg fixed, so that when he bent it down, it stayed down.

After that, my mother consented to be in the living room for his pre-working visits. But she always left the front door wide open.

"I like a breeze," she said.

~

CHAPTER 3

FAMILY LIFE

MORNING IS OUR LOVELIEST TIME

A foreign friend and I were discussing family life the other day and he brought up the fact that Americans are always portrayed in the movies as grouchy and unorganized in the mornings before breakfast.

I told him I couldn't understand where the film writers got that idea.

"You're an average American," he said. "How does your typical morning begin?"

Morning is our loveliest time, I told him.

We generally awaken around 6 a.m. with big wide smiles on our faces.

My wife remarked just this morning, after a party the night before, "Listen dear, hasn't our alarm clock a splendid tone?"

"I like the vibrato best," I said. "Reset it so we can hear it again."

Sometimes gentlemen from the sanitary engineering department will drop a garbage can under our window at 5 a.m.

We have a good laugh over this, I told him.

"It sure doesn't sound like the movies," said my friend.

Oh, there are slight differences.

I always offer to skip downstairs and start breakfast, but my wife kisses my forehead and says, "Please, dear, return to sleep. I can't wait to get into the kitchen to start the Eggs Benedict. Or would you prefer broiled trout with a sour cream sauce?"

Solely for the sake of family unity, I roll over and go back to sleep.

"How about the kids?" asked my amazed friend.

I tried to think of something unusual about their morning.

But couldn't.

They arise about 7 a.m., skip to our room and sing, *"Good morning to you, good morning to you, we're all in our places with sunshiney faces, and to you we say, have a nice day!"* and make their beds with hospital corners, and then come downstairs where they all line up and say "Good morning" to their mother and me.

After I inspect their fingernails, they usually stand around in an informal group remarking on how well each looks.

"This certainly puts a new light on American morning life," said my foreign friend. "In France, I always have trouble over the bathroom. How do you handle this?"

I told him I never really thought much about it.

Sometimes, I admitted, I have to hurry them along when the 16-year-old will stand outside the bathroom door and say to the 13-year-old, "You first, you were a hair ahead of me."

And the 13-year-old will stall and say, "No, I want to be fair about this—let's flip a coin."

After the boys are dressed they will usually ask if I have any yard work before breakfast.

Since we all have to be either at school or work by 8:30, it is difficult to oblige them.

However, they take it like good sports.

When we gather for breakfast, the five-year-old recites a poem and then we all put on paper hats and march around the table singing *You Are My Sunshine.*

"Is there anything unusual about that?" I said.

My friend said, "I'm not going to any more American movies!"

"I should think not," I said.

~

Calling people to dinner at our residence was sometime complicated, like figuring out income tax forms or discussing foreign policy.

Our chef, recognized between meals as wife and mother of our children, has a "THING" about cooking meals and every so often having no one show up to consume them while they are hot.

This "THING" is deep seated.

Carpenters also have a "THING" about building a house in which nobody comes to live.

Presidential candidates have a "THING" about running for a national office and having no one show up to vote!

This is what a "THING" is!!

One of her big problems was the dissemination of her dinner calls.

We have a big two-story white house in which dwell two Hims and a Her, almost new.

The difference between our white house and the one in Washington, D.C., is that it has servants and the head of the household can come to dinner any time he darn pleases!

Our inhabitants are holed up upstairs and usually keep radios or hi-fis blaring around dinner time. It is not uncommon to hear, *"Yar, yar ya ya ring on my finger turned green over you honey poo"* or *"The bridge's washed out, and my baby's on the other side—ya ya!"*

Downstairs I try to compete with Tchaikowski, which has lots of tympani parts.

From the church across the street, I have had it passed down that our house sounds like a Hong Kong bar!

Somehow through this foundry of cacophony, our cook must gather the clan to dinner. I have encouraged her to take up the bugle.

Modern day mothers are not the bellowers of my youth.

During my early youth in Kingsburg, California, I could hear, come supper time, my mother's call clean over at the

Bonsteel's, a block away. Or down in our gang's cave near the Thompson seedless vineyards.

She would open the back screen door and begin with a strong "G" swooping up to a high "C."

It came out like, ''WAAAAAALEEE and DONAAAALLLD'' (my brother) "DIIIINNNNEEEERR!!!!"

Sometimes, if our response was too slow, a neighbor would relay a second call.

I also had a grand Gramma who lived in the mountains over-looking the Pacific Ocean, and her back-door bellow came out, "WARRRRRRLLOOOSSSS! WOOOOOOHAAAAAA!!!"

It had Tarzan quality to it that had a ring of adventure and the old West.

If I happened to be treebound a goodly pace back in the woods, I would imagine it was Jane!

I haven't heard a good neighborhood motherly call to a meal in years.

Today's kids are confined to backyards if they go out at all.

At our Santa Cruz house, as the kids grew, my wife used the rumor system.

When someone padded through the kitchen, she would say that dinner would be ready in 35 minutes, hoping the rumor would spread. Otherwise, when time grew nigh, she would open the broom closet door and in a normal voice announce dinner.

The space was open to the second floor so the bellow became outdated.

Her routine, however, has addendums when called for.

Occasionally, as we are dealing with humans here, say four minutes pass.

"Well, if no one wants to dine, why did I bother to prepare this magnificent meal! I am going to go ahead and eat!"

Next stage: "Well, I'll have to throw the rest out."

Kids rush down to save what is left to find the food is just being served and piping hot.

"Aw, Ma!!!"

~

BED MAKING? WHAT'S THAT?

I have resigned myself that I will never make the Bed Makers' Hall of Fame.

Which is no Herculean deal, except that those of cultural bent do not take this art lightly.

Lousy bed makers have had to fight against natty factions, face ridicule, and been made to feel minor misfits of civilized society.

Those who rile against our ilk (note the "our"—ilks love company), fear, I suppose, that the beds they make they will have to lie in, or lay in, depending upon the intent. (What does that sentence mean?)

I know a few who would not hesitate to write their congresswomen, to push legislation making an unmade bed a misdemeanor (and thusly punish the bed!).

That I am a rather devil-may-care bed maker is peculiar, for I come from a strict bed-making family and have had opportunities that other boys and girls did not have.

The best instructors were at my beck and call.

But I blew it.

Through most of my youth, I left my beds like snakes leave their skins.

I never looked back.

I kept my fingernails clean, even washed behind my ears, and never blew gum bubbles in church. Didn't matter. I was given to believe that leaving a scrunched up, cover askew, rumpled bed displayed a character weakness that could fester into a life of crime.

I was even given a second chance.

There were a half-dozen sergeants during World War II who devoted a segment of their careers to trying to make a bed maker out of me.

They earnestly imparted their tricks toward the art of the hospital corner.

They stretched brown blankets across the top of my bed so tight that quarters would tango for minutes after being casually dropped thereon.

I suppose I wanted something else out of life and eventually disappointed my sergeants and my mother, and probably my country.

My hospital corners turned out like badly sutured appendixes, and when quarters were dropped on my bed, they would disappear down some deep fold.

It would take some time to find them.

And my whole barracks would have to run three times around the parade ground when we should have been preparing to fight the Nazis.

I suppose there are others like me.

Perhaps we should start a pen-pal club.

Trade photos of our worst-made beds.

I am made to feel that I should reach back into my past and come up with some traumatic experience which manifested itself in poor bed making.

Well, I, for one, am not interested in doing so.

It would only cause me to "break out," as my Gramma put it after eating too many wild blackberries.

To me, a bed which looks like goulash at mid-day symbolizes life astir.

It indicates that someone has bounded into the day with vigor, eager to get on with it.

Show me a bed which resembles a meringue pie at 3 p.m. and I'll show you an occupant who probably has his underwear on backwards—but who has a vibrant personality.

Some people make beds as if they are trying to forget the night before.

Their sheets are taut, like prissy lips.

I have been in hotel rooms where full demolition crews were needed to pry loose the covers.

I like my feet free at night; instead, I often feel like a wrapped mummy. The outline of my body looks like it has been subjected to a shrink-wrap process, like they do to vegetables.

Our current problem is that we now occupy a king-sized bed and to make it would properly require the crew it takes to cover the infield at Candlestick.

When my wife and I leave the bed together of a morning, we have worked out a routine. We bought walkie-talkies and it goes something like this.

Wife: "Okay, SL24, I'm ready on my side—over!"

Me: "I read you. I'll wave my slipper when ready—over!"

Wife: "Mayday! Mayday! You're pulling the sheets over too far—over."

Pricilla Nastyneat might sniff at the results, but I'll bet our bed has more art form than hers.

Picasso would feel right at home.

I was always after the kids to improve their bed-making and not turn out like their old man, but alas, blood is thicker than hospital corners.

~

You've heard the expression "Let's sit down to a quiet game of cards."

I have too, but such a phenomenon has not been experienced in our house, probably because we play Canasta.

And I use the word "play" as in dirty pool, hog calling, and Russian Roulette.

Canasta has been ingrained into our family's sportive tradition like touch football with the Kennedys. Only we tackle in our game.

Against the advice of experts, my wife and I play the children. We're not afraid of them at all when we team up.

We wanted to set examples of how, through cooperation, friendly team spirit, concentrative determinedness, good sportsmanship, and great fun can come from the game.

They prefer one-upmanship and victory.

It took a bit of persuasion to introduce the game into the family circle because, according to Hoyle's opening comment in explaining the game: "Canasta is a game of the rummy family."

My wife didn't like the connotation.

But one can play only so much Junior Bridge or Pick-up Straws, so we took it up.

Upon doing so we have observed that:

1. As soon as the first hand is dealt, the 12-year-old's voice rises one octave and the nine-year-old uses a tone that could only be trying for an echo.

2. The nine-year-old is easygoing and our only worry of him leaving his future wife is if she should take the discard pile.

3. One should dip their eyeballs well in boric acid before attempting to watch either of them shuffle and deal.

4. They cheat.

We have been quick to correct this. It being their impressionable age.

"There will be no hinting, suggesting, or implying to your partner what you have in your hand," I once announced sternly!

"Can I sing?" asked the 12-year-old.

"Why on earth?"

"It makes the game fun."

"If you want."

"Thanks. *Tea for two, two for tea ... Mr. Five by Five, da de da de da ... Jack and Jill went up the Hill ...*"

"You cover quite a bit of territory in one breath."

"I like singing."

The nine-year-old then took over with, *Ten Little Indians, We Three Kings of Orient Are*, and a song I am not familiar with called, *Have You Got Aces, I Got Aces, All God's Chil-un Got Aces.*

And do you know, those little devils beat us four games straight!

~

◇◇◇

If I am prematurely gray, it is partly due to my unending battle with clutter around the house, and partly due to the fact that I still have hair.

Which, after all, is better than a gray bald head.

There was a time when I could stand in the center of the living room and throw a temper tantrum.

Starting with a low growl and working up to a high howl!

This had an effect similar to that of a volunteer fire department siren.

"Pitter-patter, pitter-patter" came from all over the house and objects disappeared like a home movie run backwards.

But this is when the troops were tender.

Now, only the dog howls!

The kids move with dignity and give philosophic reasons why life is the way it is.

Clutter, I suspect, is a particular weakness in a two-story house where logistics become a major factor.

I mean when the 14-year-old, dreaming of muscles, brings his 70-pound bar bell downstairs to the yard, it seldom gets further than the kitchen on its return trip.

This is because King Kong pauses to make a milk shake and then becomes sidetracked by the bathroom mirror—thence solo back upstairs to enrich his mind with a 45 rpm rendition of *Rainy Day Woman*, yeah, yeah, yeach!

Now, a 70-pound bar bell in the kitchen is not impossible to live with if you naturally walk around like a drum major, but next the Shedder enters.

The Shedder is the 11-year-old, who considers the whole house his private clothes closet.

Unconsciously, as the headshrinker is wont to say, the Shedder senses that his jacket goes well with the decor of the kitchen tablecloth; his shirt becomes pop art over the living room divan; and his pants take squatter's rights on the towel rack behind the bathroom door.

Once upstairs, he re-clothes himself, and should the situation arise for another change, he sheds again like an Air Force C-119 dropping paratroopers.

This is amateur stuff.

Should one want to discuss Big League cluttering, one has to discuss the three-year-old daughter.

And one often does in our household.

There is nothing in this wide weird world that will drain the blood from the brain faster than the sight of a life-size doll floating face down in the bathtub.

Sometimes I lie an hour on the bathroom floor before they find me!

To color a simple red balloon it is necessary to spread 359 crayons on the dining room floor.

They do not make themselves known, when I enter at night.

Sometimes I lie two hours on the dining room floor before they find me!

I combat clutter in several ways.

I run around like Napoleon at Waterloo trying to find someone to attack it.

The resulting success can be compared to Napoleon's.

I often snivel, and running to the bathroom to wipe my eyes, find that the towel is the 11-year-old's pants.

I pick things up myself.

And find, to my amazement, that this works!

~

It was one of those days when the phone hung like a useless bauble on the wall, never clearing its metallic throat once to lure me away.

The projects were magnetized to the refrigerator door—paint the front door, bare spots on lawn, plant bulbs, towel rack, on and on.

Once I get in white tennis shoes I become highly organized, which is a disadvantage around the castle, because it means I am out of tune with my helpers.

One six-year-old and one black dog.

We move about from job to job, Indian style.

I painted the door, made neatly lettered signs to hang around it, and left for the next project.

But I am called back to take a test.

"What's that say, Daddy?" said the six-year-old, leaning against the door.

"That says wet paint!!!"

"You're right, Daddy, lookit my hands."

I passed the test.

My normal procedure for fix-it projects is two projects forward and one project back. I got out the paint again and did the door.

While I was there, the dog buried a bone in my wooden container of bulbs (project two).

I am not allowed to kick dogs.

I am a modern parent who stands there and explains.

"Well, you see, if the bone is allowed to remain in my box of daffodils, the dog will return when hungry and dig them up again."

This made sense to the dog, who sat and wagged its tail.

But the six-year-old felt it was mean to garden in containers because all the gophers in the yard will "get skinny."

What are you going to do? The 13-year-old won't let me poison them, now the six-year-old wants me to feed them. The next step, I suppose, is to round them all up, get them vaccinated for rabies and arrange individual pillows around the fireplace.

I managed to shake my tormenters by climbing to the roof to scrub the skylight.

I even hummed something from *H.M.S. Pinafore*.

This left the six-year-old and a friend free to conduct a scientific experiment.

They wanted to substantiate Sir Isaac Newton's law of gravitation by dropping rocks down the sewer ventilation pipe in the front driveway.

I went to the refrigerator and looked. Nope, nothing on my project list about unclogging a sewer outlet, but the whole household was screaming, so I wrote out an addendum—"house flooding, fix."

I had about six crises during the day. Same as the President.

Solved every one except the gophers, and lumbered into the sunset, me, the six-year-old, and the black dog with a daffodil in its mouth.

~

A visitor from Holland observed the other day how busy Americans seemed to be and asked me what the average American family did in the evening.

I said I hadn't given it much thought.

"But it's about quittin' time," I said. "Come on over to my house and observe for yourself."

When we drove into the driveway, I had to back out again because a station wagon was backing out with a surfboard sticking out the back.

We went in the house and a woman came over and kissed me.

I started to introduce my friend from Holland but the name of the woman slipped my mind.

"Honey, I'm your wife," she said.

"Of course," I said. "I thought you looked familiar."

"Is the key in the car?" she said.

"Where 'ya going?"

"I'm late for my university extension class."

"I almost forgot," I said, "but how am I going to get to my Citizens for Better Streets committee meeting tonight?"

"Jud will be back from surfing in time."

"So that was HIM. I thought this was his judo night."

"It is, a chum will pick him up."

I said I had brought my friend home for dinner and wondered what there was to eat.

"Dinner's in the oven," she said. "The five-year-old will be eating with you when she gets back."

"Piano lessons?"

"No, you took her there last night on the way to your club meeting."

"Oh."

The 14-year-old passed through the kitchen and said, "Hi, see ya."

"Neighbor kid?"

"He's yours," said my wife. "He's late for a Scout meeting."

"Oh, yeah, I remember. He and I were home together two weeks ago last Wednesday. He told me all about himself."

The five-year-old came in from playing at the neighbor's house.

Her mother said, "Will you please set the table for your father?"

"Sure. Hi, Dad," she said to the man from Holland. "No, I'm your father!" I said.

The man from Holland said, "I feel exhausted. Do you mind if I sit down?"

I said, "You certainly may. Let me take the dust covers off the chairs."

"What would happen," said the man from Holland, "if one of your classes or meetings is called off?"

I said, "I guess every family has experienced this problem. If a family isn't prepared, it can throw it completely off schedule."

"How do you guard against this?" he said.

"Each member is expected to have an alternate plan," I said. "For example, if my street meeting should be cancelled, I am also a member of the curbs and gutters committee, which is also meeting tonight. If the 14-year-old's Scout meeting is postponed, his bowling team is rolling tonight."

"I think I understand," said the man. "It's a wonderful idea, and I have decided on my alternate plan for tonight."

"What's that?"

"The 11 p.m. flight back to Holland!"

~

The family is waiting, with great suspense, its grade in relief map making.

The grade actually will be posed in the name of the nine-year-old who came home with an assignment to create California in flour, salt, and water.

He was up to his elbows in dough, creating the most crowded state in the union, when the 12-year-old wandered by and casually mentioned that Carquinez strait was askew.

And gave San Francisco Bay a poke.

Completely obliterating Alcatraz Island.

My wife shooed him away, then happened to notice that San Joaquin Valley was a trifle too long.

But restrained herself from any action.

"If San Joaquin Valley is too long, fix it," I said.

"It's his project," she said. "He'll learn by doing."

"Well, he's learning to make Death Valley too high. It's supposed to be below sea level," I said, dabbing at Death Valley with my forefinger, lowering it 40 to 50 feet.

"Daddy," said the nine-year-old, vexed, "you've pushed the San Bernardino mountains into Los Angeles."

He pushed them back, filling in part of the Salton Sea. But I held back from re-dredging it.

He must learn by doing.

"Parents should not do their children's homework," scolded the 12-year-old, frowning disapproval because the Coast Range was too close to the sea.

"You're not giving Santa Cruz any room to be Santa Cruz," he told the nine-year-old, ignoring his own advice to his parents and pushing Loma Prieta back toward San Jose.

"Let's all go away and let him work," said my wife.

This would have ended our consultation had I not noticed that the Sierras between Yosemite and Mt. Whitney were FAR too low.

I've pulled a burro through this country and its towering grandeur is its power.

So, when the nine-year-old wasn't looking, I gave the Sierra Nevada a pinch, uplifting them 500 feet.

"That's far too high," said my wife, who spotted the movement through special eyes she maintains in the back of her head.

She walked over and squished at least 200 miles of Sierra back down again.

"It's ridiculous," I said. "Mt. Whitney's now lower than Half Dome."

The nine-year-old was persuaded to squeeze Mt. Whitney up a bit.

During dinner someone sneaked into the family room and gave Whitney a quick disapproving pat.

Between dessert and coffee I managed to make Whitney craggy again. By bedtime, California took on a strong resemblance to Montana.

Finally my wife put her foot down and we all went away and the nine-year-old got California back.

The next morning I noticed, before he left for school, that Carquinez strait was askew again.

He saw me biting my nails.

"That's the way I like Carquinez strait," he said.

~

There is a history of somniloquy in my family which runs back to President Tyler and probably farther.

It has consistently favored the female side for a reason not yet known, but what is known is that this sleep-talking has been a powerful force in their hands and has reduced more than one of our males to neurotic shambles.

I do not imagine that people normally record such peculiarities within the family, but we are also letter savers and the subject has been threaded throughout many an old correspondence.

I recall coming across the fearsome phrase in a letter from Aunt Rachael to my grandfather Clint: "I hear Pete is marrying an upstate girl. I wonder if she will be a night talker."

This was not taken lightly by the males in our strain; any unexplained factor in one's life tends to work on the nervous system and hair-line. We have been nervous as far back as anyone can remember, mainly due to what our women say at night.

When somniloquy is discussed at family reunions, someone always brings up my Aunt Clara in Cincinnati who would suddenly sit bolt upright in bed, deep in the night, and shout, "TAKE IT, CHARLIE!"

She had a voice that could rip curtains!

My uncle was afflicted with the sort of nervousness that made Don Knotts famous, and when Aunt Clara yelled, "Take it, Charlie," he would leap out of bed, waving his arms like one wildly clearing away spider webs, and sputter, "Whazzzit, Clara?"

Both would end up standing beside the bed in their nightgowns until one of them suggested they "git back in bed."

Aunt Clara would slump back to sleep leaving her husband staring wide-eyed into the blackness, twitching slightly around the mouth.

The next morning they would discuss the incident over breakfast, but Aunt Clara could never remember anything, or at least, this was her story.

These episodes kept eating away at my uncle, mainly, I suppose, because his name was not Charlie.

It was Ben.

Uncle Ben would write long, painful letters to my father and mother, and I used to hear them discussing the problem quite thoroughly with the letter lying before them on the kitchen table.

Once my mother suggested that perhaps Aunt Clara had, in her youth, led a jazz band and was used to shouting at "Charlie" to take a solo on whatever instrument he played.

But my father did not remember his sister ever leading a jazz band.

He did say, however, that she once played the organ in her church, and this brought up the possibility that Aunt Clara might have yelled, "TAKE IT, CHARLIE!" to the minister.

After finishing her pre-sermon hymn.

But no one took it seriously.

As with most of the husbands in our lineage, Uncle Ben never discovered to his satisfaction who Charlie was and whenever our families got together, I remember Ben as a wrinkled, bent man, given to talking to himself.

Aunt Clara seemed the stronger of the two and was forever helping Uncle Ben up curbs.

I can discuss Ben's case now, for he has gone on to more serene pastures where one hopes that his sleep is undisturbed.

In the meantime, the rest of us are carrying on the best we can.

~

THE HALLOWEENING OF UNCLE ED

I suppose this is as good a time as any to dwell on a family story concerning the Halloweening of my Uncle Ed out of Omaha.

Uncle Ed was a staid man, set in his ways, the type who would become extremely upset if served soup for breakfast. He voted for William Howard Taft.

He was an excitable man who used dignity as a crutch and never removed his tie at night until undressing for bed.

As my mother used to tell it, Uncle Ed disliked Halloween as Ebenezer Scrooge disliked Christmas, and he would always retire early on this eve, leaving Harriet, his wife, to answer the door for the trick or treaters.

It was Harriet who baked the cookies and carved the pumpkin for the front door stoop. That year it was a huge vegetable. She conventionalized it with triangle eyes and a sweeping grin.

Uncle Ed had converted himself with a long nightgown and red night cap with a dangling black ball and had hied himself upstairs to bed at dusk.

It is unclear in our family how it came about, I mean, how the pumpkin became stuck on Aunt Harriet's head.

Perhaps it had been the result of a fantasy she had of winning first prize at a costume ball, or maybe it had somehow fallen. Whatever it was, it had squeezed down over her head and it had become stuck with the upside down face now frozen in a deep frown.

Her view was limited to the triangled nose opening and the weight of the pumpkin caused her to reel drunkenly about the room.

A covey of youngsters approached the front door, took one look in unison in a side window and had fled in a chorus of screams.

Uncle Ed had been reading by the dim bedside lamp and was in that never-never land between consciousness and sleep when he heard an inhuman beseechment and an unsteady thumping on the stairs, growing in intensity.

It was Harriet, of course, frantically calling for help. Her legs were bowed from the weight, her arms were flailing about for support, and there were considerable hysterics being emitted through the nose of the pumpkin.

Now, after a traumatic event is over, everyone can sit around speculating over how it could have been better handled.

Our family has discussed this, and we generally have concluded that Harriet should have knocked before entering Uncle Ed's bedroom. But, as I say, we were not there.

The approaching clamor was frightening enough, but when Aunt Harriet burst into the room and stood there silhouetted against the eerie hallway light, Uncle Ed froze for the better half of a micro-second, then seemed to levitate from his bed.

Aunt Harriet tried to make sense, I am sure, and cried out from within her soggy echo chamber, "Sur lime a some!"

Uncle Ed's panicking brain interpreted this as meaning, "Your time has come!" It is told that the man, now standing on the bed, eased into a sort of a semi-crouch, then leaped clean out of the open bedroom window, landing on Harriet's boxwood bush, "without," as he put it later, "feeling a thing."

Uncle Ed was not a coward. My mother used to say he had the makin's of a brave man, but I suppose every man has his limits.

Lying spread-eagle on the rose bush, it entered the unfrozen section of his brain that Aunt Harriet was still in the house with the beast with the upside-down face.

He made a brave dash for the front door only to find himself among about six sheet-clad tots awaiting an answer to their knock and squinting into the side window by the door.

Their answer was a hopping, staggering, arm-waving, pumpkin-headed figure coming toward them.

A neighbor was later to report what he considered to be a newsworthy sight to the local press.

The story told of a group of little kids in Halloween costumes chasing an elderly man in a nightgown down the street.

"They were moving at a rate of speed quite astounding, considering the ages of both parties," said the neighbor.

~

"Which is more important to you, the moon or your infant child?" asked my wife at 2:14 p.m. Sunday in a tone not unlike that used by the chairman of the House Un-American Activities Committee.

This was not a propitious question.

It had needles in it.

I answered her silently with a look unique in the facial muscular structure of men married 18 years.

She read the look like one with eyes skilled at Braille, and took the floor again.

"You pay good taxes to have 7,000 photographs taken of the moon, but you haven't spent a cent for film to snap your own daughter. Not in a moon's age!"

"I think you meant coon's age, dear!"

"Don't you get smart-alecky with me! Which is more important to you, the moon ..."

"Cease, cease," I cut in. "I dig your analogy, but, you see, the moon is something rather new to science, and ..."

"Your child is new, too—newer than the moon by a long shot!" she blasted off.

That statement had the nuts and bolts of a smart-alecky repartee.

But inasmuch as my wife had received her Black Belt a week ago Tuesday, I soft-pedaled and merely opined that it was a little late to write the government for a refund on my share of the moon shot now!

"Don't get smart-alecky," she ordered.

We have photographs of our goldie-locks—so many, in fact, that if we stapled them together and thumbed them fast it would run longer than *Gone With The Wind*.

She's so used to being photographed by her parents that when I skip a few months, she stops growing. And waits!

If our bunting hadn't such a moon face, I don't think my luv would have made such a comparison with this current moon shot to get her point across, but when she gloms onto a subject it's like trying to avoid radar.

"If you were a loving father," she continued, finding her second wind, "you'd get out our Ranger 8 and make with the shutter of your daughter while she's still cute on the hobby horse!"

"What on earth are we going to do with 7,000 photos of her on a hobby horse!" I asked askedly.

"Well," she retorted, chin out, "There's Aunt Martha, Grampa Julius, bubble gum cards ..."

"And," I continued, "she might run for president some day on the Democratic ticket and we can pass them out to show she was partial to the donkey ever since her hobby horse days."

So I went out and clicked a few snaps of the infant—starting at 25 feet and continued to clickity-click until the camera crashed into her head, around the Sea of Pores on her forehead.

We haven't had time to completely analyze the prints as yet, so I cannot report how deep the surface of her skin is.

But, unlike the moon's suspected soft surface, all of us have made quite a few lip landings on the high ridges of her cheek, and I can report that they are firm and receivable.

~

FLOWER POWER OF THE BANJO

The banjo, scientists will be all agog to know, has flower power.

There is nothing like *Sweet Georgia Brown* in F to make a primrose sit up and take notice.

"Plunkety plunk!"

The 13-year-old has a school science experiment under way that will determine how much music affects the growth of a plant.

Will identical plants, put to the same soil, respond to different kinds of music?

Will they survive?

Science not withstanding, my question is, "Will we survive?"

Upstairs , in his room, one primrose is engaged in Mendelssohn at full volume!

Will it develop long hair?

Downstairs in the living room, another is subjected to, *"Yea! Yea! Yeah!"* whilst listening to The Kitchen Sinks.

Will it develop the "twist"?

In the study I am plunking the banjo to a shuddering flower. But it is paying rapt attention.

Which is more than I can say about the rest of the family when I play. But back to the subject at hand.

It is the 13-year-old's theory that the vibrations from the music will stir botanic juices.

His experiment does not take into consideration how all this is affecting the household's human juices.

My wife uses ear plugs which I bravely understand with only a slight wavering of the lower lip.

And I admit the house vibrates with a cacophony of inhuman sounds that can only erupt from an elementary school band in the agonizing throes of "warming up"!!!

RUM RUM, RUM, YEAH! YEAH!, PLUNKETY PLUNK PLUNK.

On theory, one primrose is not supposed to hear what the

other primroses are hearing, but doors are often left open and they get, *"Yeah, yeah, my baby don love me no mo,"* mixed with *Midsummer Night's Dream* and a smattering of *Banjo Rag.*

Excedrin pills are eating themselves!!

But I have been compensated somewhat by the boy's findings.

"Daaad, you've got flower power!!!!"

Heavens to Betsy!

My banjo serenaded primrose blossoms as healthy as a yogi at a health spa where the others have that "Thank God it's Friday" look.

If the 13-year-old's studies are valid, I can visualize a grand revival of *If You Knew Suzy Like I Know Suzy* and the *Darktown Strutters Ball* coming from every nursery.

Meanwhile I hope that Mendelssohn has rubbed off on the 13-year-old.

When my wife heard that my banjo had such a beneficial effect on the primrose, she brightened more than a little bit.

"Wonderful!!! From now on you can banjo out in the garden!"

I think I've been bamboozled!

~

DON'T PUT THE CAR AWAY!

I am a father chauffeur. I am married to a mother chauffeur. We drive our offspring around town, tra la, tra la, to their endless activities.

"Don't put the car away, Daaad, this is Scout night."

"Why can't you walk?"

"Because you have to take me to junior choir practice first, and I can't go to Scouts in my choir robe. Can I?"

"I thought Scouts are supposed to be brave as well as clean and reverent!"

Our engine seldom cools. Thither and yon we go.

Often we will meet other parents going yon.

"Dad, I have to go to play practice, and I'm late. Can you run me over?"

When we were young, we used legs to walk or bike.

But over the years something went cattywappus.

Sometime, when your kids are dressing, take a close look and you will find only a vestige of legs!

I asked our Scout why he didn't hike over to his meet like a good Scout?

"Because that doesn't count toward my hiking merit badge."

"Oh."

A request comes in for a short ride to an afternoon dance class.

But it was only three blocks away. Only three blocks?

I mumbled that, "I used to walk 2 miles to school when I was your age."

That won points until my wife told the children, "He lived next to the school located on Two Mile Road."

She said she would have to wear "my best dress, and kids don't walk in the streets in their GOOD clothes!! What if I saw someone I knew?"

Father and mother chauffeurs have their own tribal chants: "You take him this time."

"All right but I made the last run."

"All right, I'LL take him."

"No, you're tired, I'll do it."

"Don't be silly."

"Okay, you go ahead and take him, I wanted to watch boxing."

Sometimes we are double whammed! Especially around baseball season.

"Daaad, can you pick up Joey, Phil, and Alex? Their parents are booked by other kids in their families."

Many parents who go thither and yon have nodding acquaintances with other thither and yon parents. But only from the head.

I probably know a couple of dozen from the neck up. Everything else is blocked by the car body. I don't know if they are fat, thin or svelte, or lumpy. They could be naked for all I know.

Oh, if fat kids emerged one might picture a plump parent. But you never know.

At popular destinations our cars entwine like a motorized May pole dance. If someone set up loud speakers, with a bit of practice, we might work out some doe-zee-doe moves!!!

Once a schedule had been established, the young minds start comparing automobiles.

The status factor sets in. "Dad, can you bring the new car next time?"

"Pete's Dad brings him in a red convertible every time!"

"I've heard he uses snuff and chug-a-lugs Shirley Temples."

The daughter also frowns on my wearing my old comfortable yard sweater. She asked me not to wear it if I pick her up from a party.

I say, "Now what difference does it make what I wear? No one will ever see me unless I have to come to the door to let you know I am waiting!"

"DON'T YOU DARE!!"

~

"I don't see why we keep feeding the cat," I uttered to my wife a morning-and-a-half ago. "He doesn't acknowledge our existence."

This morning I found a note near Streaker's food dish.

"Dear Keeper—notice I do not use 'buddy,' nor 'master,' nor 'mentor', and the 'dear' is strictly platonic:

"I do not make a practice to communicate with my keepers, but that crack you made a morning-and-a-half ago about feeding me levitated my thoracic vertebrates.

"I do not acknowledge your existence, sir, because I am shown no respect nor love from anyone around here.

"I am not just any cat. I come highly educated, holding a BA from Catawaba College, a Master's from Catlina U, and nine PhDs from Nine Lives Correspondence School.

"I hate to be catty about it, but, I understand you have only one degree, and to what degree you use it, I shudder to cogitate.

"How do you expect me to respond favorably when:

"1. You feed me near Goldie The Dog, ignoring the fact that this fat slob of a canine balloon will veer over to my dish when she one-swallows the contents of her dish. She almost mistook my head for a bone the other morning.

"2. You expect me to curl in front of the fireplace for atmosphere when you have company, not caring that I am overheating like an Indian inside his ceremonial sweat lodge.

"3. You coo, 'it's sooooo cute' when the dog comes over and licks my face with her tongue. Obviously, you've never been slapped with a wet blanket that's been dipped in leftover ALPO.

"4. Once in a great while I make a mess in the hallway. Instead of showing empathy, you react as if I laid a deposit of nuclear waste on the floor—in spite.

"5. You never gave me a chance to be a sex object. You had me catrated, or whatever you call it.

"6. You keep making snide remarks about my not earning my keep by catching gophers in the garden. I do not go for gophers. I am nonviolent. I once helped a mole across the street.

"7. When you let me in the house, you come excruciatingly close to closing the front door on my tail. There is five more inches of me after my butt clears the threshold.

"Should it ever happen, I have a cry that'll spin the buttons off your long johns. I also hold in reserve a cry that sounds precisely like a wife being throttled by her husband. It will destroy your already shaky reputation in these parts.

"How do you expect me to respond lovingly if I am not welcome to jump on your bed for a warm sleep at night?

"So I miss sometimes in the dark and land on your face. With a face like yours, a little alteration would help.

"All I get is a kick.

"When I sleep outdoors, I come serenading at your bedroom window for my breakfast at a reasonable hour, and what do I get for my first course? Your brown hiking boot—airborne.

"Do you know what time I get up? You two just keep on sawing away until 6 a.m. The day is practically over by then, and I starve.

"Other cats around here think I have anorexia.

"Another thing.

"When I am out there in the night protecting the place from every Tom, Tom, and Tom, I expect a little appreciation.

"When you can shape up and resolve the above matters, we will try again.

"P.S. I do not like generic canned cat food."

~

CHAPTER 4

TRAVELS

THE TRAIL TALKER

Bear Paw Meadows: The 12-year-old is bent under his backpack; our trail is murderously steep, like current food prices, and movement is gut-straining. But I know he hasn't given up because he is still talking.

"Man, it's hot!"

"I must have got rocks in my pack!"

"Lookit that great canyon!"

"When are we going to get there?"

Ten thousand feet, with scarcely enough atmosphere to fill the lungs of a skinny gnat, but the 12-year-old talks on.

Every time he asks me if I'm tired, I get tireder!

We plunge over high rocky ridges, clomp down into fern-cool meadows, switch back up through hot, dusty August forests, snaking with the endless trail which shows no hint of a destination.

I consult the map frequently; I reek with confidence. I am a leader, until the Trail Talker asks, "Are we on the right trail?"

This immediately plunges me into serious doubt.

Will they find our bones, come spring?

The 12-year-old is also a Pointer-Outer.

That granite peak to my left matches perfectly with the one on the map, confirming our whereabouts, until he points out that what I am looking at on the map is actually a canyon.

Kerplunk, back to panic!

What I identify as a common mountain bush snake and stoop to pet is pointed out by the 12-year-old as an eight-button Diamond back rattler.

Sending me screaming 3 feet off the ground!

Nor does the Trail Talker give up at long distances.

He loves to chat across switchback trails or from mountain tops.

"Caaaaan yooooouuu heeaaaaarrrr mmmeeeeeeee?"

Is the child in trouble?

"Whaaaaat doooooo yoooouuuu waaaaannnnt??" I thunder back. "Doooooo youuuuuuuu neeeeeeeeed heelllllllp?"

"I juuuuussssssstttt waaaaaanaannnt tooooo knooooooooow if youuuuuuuuuuuu caaaaaaaan heeeeeeeeeeeeeearrrrrrrrrrr meeeeeeee!"

This is exhausting.

The child is full of small talk at this distance.

I yearn for the solid quietness of the Sierra above the tree line, where the rocks reflect the hard void.

Each word saved in this rare atmosphere is three steps earned, I say.

He unleashed a litany of "what ifs."

"What if a bear got all our food and we got lost and I broke my leg and you got sick and it rained and a rock slide blocked our way out and we lost our map?" asks the Trail Talker cheerily.

However, soon the magnificent glory of the grand scenery wipes any negative thought from our freshly rejuvenated minds.

~

In this dream the other night I was standing before a tribunal and the judge was growling, "I will give you a choice in your sentence—take a long auto trip with your kids, or join the Marines in the jungles of Vietnam."

In the next dream scene there is a sound of mortar fire and whining of bullets and I am humming and prancing merrily into the jungles, clicking my heels in the air.

In reality, though, these auto trips must be faced.

"Dat rat it, quit throwing things!"

"Stop hitting your sister, or I'll bla, bla, bla, bla, bla, bla!"

This is America crisscrossing the summer country having fun.

Hi ho and away we go toward vacation-land—with one hand on the wheel and the other waving frantically at the tigers in the back.

"Quit dragging your arms outside the car, Philbert, or we'll turn right around and ..."

In the olden days (45 B.C. to the kids) autos were more cramped, slower, and the sun made X-rays through the isinglass.

Nowadays our children have a half-acre in the back of the station wagon and KMBY (heaven help us all) and Kleenex to blow their noses in.

"GET REX FROM UNDER THE DASH BEFORE HE ELECTROCUTES HIMSELF!!!"

We have solved a goodly part of these territorial motorized conflicts with car games.

There are several that have clung to our group which I even enjoy.

One is the alphabet sign game.

One person or party takes the signs on the right side of the road; the other takes those on the left.

First side to reach "z" first by picking the letters from the signs wins.

The driver, unless he is an ardent fatalist, should shy away from this game.

Another good one is "Who am I?"

One person thinks of a personality—say Phyllis Diller—and the rest of the mob in the car tries to guess the name by quizzing him. The person "it" must answer correctly.

Is the person male? Is she an author? Is she alive?"

Gradually the clues pile up and the facts are narrowed down to the answer.

This game usually keeps order between Hollister and Fresno. The one who guesses Phyllis Diller is "it," don't you see?

Those who have jolly good memories like to play this elimination game.

Someone starts out: "I went to London and took along my bathing cap."

The next one follows: "I went to London and took along my bathing cap and Beatles records." Each party adds one item, but he must remember all the previous items mentioned, and the list continues to grow until all but the winner are eliminated by forgetting one of the items.

Another time-consumer involves cold, hard cash on father's part, but it's worth it.

Name a list of items for which you will pay one cent for each sighting—like a Greyhound bus, plane in the air, windmills, hawk, rabbit, deer, phone booth, bicycle, train, etc.

Stay clear of tractors, cows, sheep, stop signs, planes on the ground and such things or you'll end up wiring your bank for money, for sure as Ned you'll round a curve and find a million sheep on the move, or pass an airport during an air show.

It takes practice to choose items that come infrequently enough to keep the kids interested.

~

I WILL GET THROUGH, I WILL, I WILL

King's Canyon National Park: Ski tracks join my clodhopper snowshoe impressions—arcing in gracefully from the forest above and disappearing ahead in neat twin ribbons.

I am on a dramatic mission.

I must get through!

I will get through; I will. I will!

It has been snowing for days, bending the tree branches to their trunks until they appear as giant white tenpins; frosting the cabin roof like a Christmas cake.

There is a padded quietness in the air; in the dells, falling snow is as gentle as a mother caressing her baby.

The sky is a slate and everything is deadly beautiful.

And if the man on skis got through—so can I!

This is a lonely mission with a half-mile to go.

I am satisfied with my solitude, for I have a Charlie Chaplin gait on snowshoes and no one would take me seriously!

Waddle, clomp; waddle, clomp; waddle, clomp!

Back at the cabin the family huddles and waits. Snow is to the windowsills and the eaves are edged with icicles, like long teeth from some winter monster in the act of swallowing the building!

Snow is everywhere; ridged along the top of the iron water pump handle; humped over the woodpile, rapidly healing the scars where we have dug for chunks of oak.

And the fires are going; strong red flames, licking at the coldness.

And there is a close mustiness inside and in the bedrooms you can smell the winter quilts.

We are usually very careful.

But a crisis arose.

I did not flinch an instant.

Against the tearful pleading of my woman, I dressed against the storm and strapped on snowshoes.

Then, opening the door just enough to slip through, I faded into the curtain of whiteness, forearm o'er forehead to ward off the stinging blasts of wind!

A man must be a man, even if he does walk like Charlie Chaplin on snowshoes.

Down through the ages man has had to act when his family finds itself in dire need.

And my family is in trouble.

But, fear not, I am on my way for help.

To the Wilsonia mountain store for a quart of milk so we can get on with making pancakes for breakfast!!

~

I am sitting at 7,000 feet in my camping togs, dwelling philosophically on where I failed in the packing of the car.

"We take only the essentials," I announced sternly the morning before we left, and then went to work.

My leaving touched off a wild stampede.

I doubt if Eisenhower, in planning his strategy for D-day, put as much effort into his project as my two young passengers.

My wife, being enceinte, decided to spend a glorious week of rest at home.

I now figure my first flaw was in neglecting the language barrier.

The difference in their connotation of "essentials" and mine was about 500 pounds.

How, for example, could one spend a week in the Sierras without the dog?

Therefore, it followed, that the dog's bare essentials were its plastic bathtub, dog soap, flea powder, brush, and 10 cans of dog food.

Well then, if the 10-year-old got to bring his dog, the eight-year-old would be justified in bringing his cat.

Therefore, it followed that the cat's bare essentials would be the cat box, its scratch pad, and 10 cans of cat food.

Next came essential mountain equipment, which included flashlights (five?), two hiking sticks, one canoe paddle, bats, balls, gloves, a mouse trap, three cans of Band-Aids, 14 collection jars, bongo drums, three play rifles, and a homemade apple box-roller skates scooter.

Toys? Well, in one corner of the living room it looked like Christmas morning. I was surprised they hadn't thought of their electric train set.

They also were asked to bring down from their rooms the clothing they thought they would need. This resulted in a wardrobe sufficient for a change every two hours for a week.

When I walked in that evening my first impression was that my wife had sold the house and that all our worldly possessions had been assembled in the living room awaiting the movers.

"You've got enough stuff here to fill a van," I stormed at the kids, each standing defiantly in front of his pile of essentials, "and it'll use up your whole vacation just unloading it."

"Now dear," said my wife, attorney for the defense, before her rigged jury of two, "if you really try I think you can tuck most of these things into spare corners of the trunk."

"How do you tuck a 24-inch Western Flyer bicycle with rack and light?" I asked.

They relented on this item, but altogether too easily, leaving strewn along their retreating path the suspicion that the bike was a plant, a clever decoy, a planned blow to the soft underbelly.

So I became an uncompromising shyster, dreaming up National Park Law 14,958 which forbids dogs and cats in the area; Law 394,878 which says that bongo drums are not allowed because the beat drives the deer into doing the Twist which is unseemly and un-deer-like.

The kids had not prepared a workable argument in defense of one canoe paddle, so I won that verdict also.

Finally I hewed the paraphernalia down to automobile size, leaving just enough room for myself and the pouting jury. We departed with the back wheels barely showing.

And now, sitting here pensively around the ol' campfire, amid nature's forest folk, I've been trying to puzzle out how the 10-year-old managed to tuck 15 pounds of weightlifting equipment into the tuckless trunk.

And where and why six cans of dog food made the ride.

And most of all, how I failed to spot the electric train, 15 feet of track and one automatic wig-wag signal.

～

Pear Lake: It's the perfect backpack trips that you don't remember. It hailed up here the first day. Great gobs of baby fat, how it hailed!

The Sierra storm dunked us like doughnuts. It sopped the camp. And at nearly 10,000 feet, wood is scarce. And all the scarce wood was wet.

Wet, like the four glum souls huddled like hunchbacks under a gnarled white-bark pine, misshaped by winds and winter snows.

We rigged a plastic lean-to to keep the sleeping bags dry, but flash riverlets sought them out—and found them.

Thunder rolled in like trucks racing over loose bridge boards and the hail made the lake waters dance.

Well, these are the elements and they baby no one.

Our campfire fought back like a David battling Goliath and finally won because of the concentrated pitch in the wood.

Pear Lake is a snow lake caught in a rocky alpine basin above the tree line in Sequoia National Park. Its overflow tumbles down the canyon to add status to the Kaweah River headwaters, rushing over pure rock with the frothy vigor of youth.

The lake is a mere dot below mighty 11,000-foot Alta Peak, smeared with snowfields.

I guess the rain chased most of the packers out of the back country, for we had the lake to ourselves.

But the joke was on them, because when it stopped raining, it was warm and fine and the vim returned in the kids and, with all this magnificent grandeur around us, we drank hot vegetable soup.

And the trout were positively indecent in their greediness to get at our hooks.

The 11-year-old and his friend Patty, also 11, scored first in the lake and assured us fish for breakfast, and their lusty choruses of, "Dad, I got one ... Whooopeeeee!!" zinged through the clean virgin air.

Bud Jones, local masonry contractor, is the rugged fisherman of our group.

He drew out 18 trout the first two days—his pole and line and techniques seem native to the spot where he stands.

I am a spider fisherman. When I cast, I weave my line around my neck, through several shrubs, under sunken logs, and once I have flung it, my mind moves on to other fields.

So that if an absent-minded trout should take my hook, I often find it digested before I am aware a fish is on the line.

I can see my 11-year-old is made from the same cut. He has moved his sleeping bag down to the rocky lake side; his line has been cast and all I can see of him is head, and, well, what are you going to do with a kid like that?

That night, we put the sleeping bags on a flat sloping rock so the rain would not form pools around us.

But the storm clouds moved away at night, as they often do in the Sierra, and we looked up at an immense spread of stars and at one point watched someone's satellite move slowly across the blackness and run smack through the bottom of the Big Dipper.

Another storm brewing—clouds as black as our kettle bottoms—so we loaded our packs the next day, rolled up the sleeping bags, cleaned camp, and hit the trail.

We made our way around a peak to another lake a mile away where the clouds seemed thinner.

We made camp on Lake Emerald, set in an amphitheater of alps, shaped like the console of those old-fashioned theater organs.

Our camp sat where the conductor might stand, and this camp was good, and while we built up a rock fireplace and scouted for wood, the kids sat down on their bags and counted 37 waterfalls cascading down the amphitheater from the snow-fields above in a lovely landscaping arrangement of moss, rock, and wildflowers that only nature could manage.

The lake gave us a double exposure of all this, broken only by the wavy rings of jumping trout.

My feet are sore, but my eyes aren't.

So let my feet complain—the "eyes" have it.

I was watching with admiration the other morn a truck and trailer back into a side street. Straight and true moved the trailer.

I never experienced straight and true days when I was pulling a travel trailer yon and thither.

Backing up is high math to me. So, even if you've only dreamed of pulling a trailer on a vacation, you should listen up.

I was telling an acquaintance on the verge just the other day, "You are entering a fretty world. Let me frighten you further by relating our first trip trailer pull, oodles of years ago."

BT (before trailering) the only thing I ever backed up was me, during a game of Simon Says.

You will find, however, everybody who owns a recreational vehicle will be eager as pie to give hints on backing.

I got free advice all the way through Canada.

"See, you place your hand at the bottom of the steering wheel and turn the wheel in the direction you wish the trailer to turn."

It was uttered to me a hundred times by a hundred personages except one man with a twitch I met at the KOA campground in Ashland, Oregon.

He said, "To hell with it. I never back a trailer. If you ever find yourself trapped in dead-end street, SELL IT! I've sold two already."

"Yes," I told my friend on the verge of entering the trailer whirl, "I tried the hand-at-the-bottom-of-the-steering-wheel, but the formula went awry."

In RV parks, backing into hookup slots, I've managed to work the trailer and car into geometric angles that would have astounded Euclid.

After parking at one slot near Banff, the manager rushed out with a camera.

Almost out of breath, he said, "You're the only party I've ever seen who can step from his car into his trailer without touching the ground!!"

I allowed, "I guess I cut 'er too sharp."

"A mite," he said. "Tell me, are you folks coming or leaving?!"

My trailer backing had people nudging each other everywhere we went.

Once I was nearly arrested on the California side of the Nevada border for promoting gambling.

A sheriff's deputy spotted a knot of recreational vehicle owners betting quite heavily on the nearest number to 20 tries it would take me to back into my space.

I was working on my 18th try when the car ran out of gas.

My wife used to help before her nervous breakdown. But actually she was a bit too emotional to be effective.

One time she stood behind the trailer yelling, "Turn away from me."

I leaned out, craning my neck.

"Where the devil are you?"

"YOU'VE GOT ME PINNED TO THE HOOKUP POWER POLE, YOU FOOL!!"

I told my friend that, for a time, we had another signal problem.

My wife used to stand toward the rear and yell out, "Swing it a bit east."

"Move eastward," she'd yell.

Now, all I know about east is that it's toward China.

With sweat rolling down the end of my nose and the trailer's right wheel on top of the site's barbecue, I'd be in no mood for geography.

So we avoided compass points, and I told my wife to signal with her arms to the right or the left.

And because when I scrooched around to look, her left would be my right. This confused me, so I asked her to stand with her back to me so we would both be going in the same direction.

This didn't work either, because an incoming rig followed her instructions and took the space.

The driver said, "Thank you, lady—you're a peach!"

~

CHAPTER 5

KIDS

MOVIE REVIEW

I was asked the other day to take a child of mine to the press showing of a children's movie, *Willy McBean and His Magic Machine*, at the Rio and to record her reaction as the film unfolded.

It may be the makings of a new form of journalistic film reviewing.

The only one of my children available to me that afternoon was the three-year-old female.

According to my notes, here is her reaction to *Willy McBean and His Magic Machine*.

Observation: "Child arrived neatly dressed, hair brushed, knees washed. Very pretty (unofficial observation); sitting primly on seat with hands in lap."

The 96-minute film was made by stop-motion photography using 100 36-inch stringless puppets.

It opens in Rasputin Von Rotten's storm-battered castle.

The mad scientist has invented a time machine. It is his scheme to go back and change history to his selfish advantage.

I liked it right away. But my opinion is not being sought.

Official observation: "Child playing with fully extended tongue!"

Counter balancing the mad, bad Von Rotten is Pablo, a talking monkey, and a little boy named Willy McBean. Pablo swiped the time machine plans and the boy built one like Von Rotten's and they set off to make history.

Very well done story line.

Official observation: "Child has skirt over head playing jack-in-the-box."

The puppets are hand-carved and ball-jointed so that the positions of each character were changed fractionally for each photograph taken. This makes them move realistically.

It took three years to make the movie. Quite delightful.

Official observation: "Child has removed shoes and stockings and is dropping same over back of seat!"

The story line is historical. Von Rotten flashes back to Tombstone and attempts to out-draw Buffalo Bill, but Pablo and Willy out-trick him, thus keeping history intact.

Characters often break out in song, musical style. Well done.

Official observation: "Child jack-knifed into seat; only bottoms of bare feet showing!"

Bad Von Rotten next goes back to Columbus year with a plan to beat him to America, but Willy and Pablo outsmart him again.

Very refreshing to see an intelligently created children's movie.

Official observation: "Child not in sight—not even feet. Man in row behind hands her back!"

Mean old Von Rotten now tries to pull the sword from the stone before Arthur and become king; when this fails he goes further back in time to become King Tut's architect.

Each time Willy and Pablo show up to save history. The musical pace is fast to keep up with young restless attention spans.

Official observation: "Child picking nose with both index fingers!"

Von Rotten finally loses his time machine in the caveman era, and Willy agrees to bring him back to the present if he promises to reform. The film then splashes color to its conclusion.

Official observation: "Child standing on seat sticking button in my right ear!"

My critical evaluation of the film is that three-year-olds are not ready for *Willy McBean and His Magic Machine*.

~

The conversation turned to allowances for children.

There was fear and tremor in their voices.

As a veteran of all this, I understood, and spaketh thusly.

An astute economist (me) once said that if the allowance system for American children ever collapsed, the nation would slump into a depression that would make the 1929 crash seem like Christmas.

Next to milk, money is the most important nourishment to the American child.

The first animal he takes to is a pig with a long slit in the back.

Under our capitalistic system, heaven forbid that one should issue a straight "no" to an appeal for an allowance. According to child psychologists this would leave them scarred for life.

So, I dwelt in fear and trembling like you folks.

Here is my method.

I explain the family budget.

I let the kids play with my bankbook (educational toy). Then I took them on a tour to back up the bankbook's claim, through my closet, pointing out the shiny areas of my trousers and the frayed cuffs on my shirts.

I don't wear these—they are decoys.

I showed them the PG&E bill and tried to look as hollow-eyed as possible.

When you think a kid is properly cowed, you suggest an, ah, modest weekly allowance, pointing out, with true justification, that you are not the Ford Foundation.

This may work until the kid compares his or her allowance with that of his friends.

"How come George gets a dollar a week and I only get 50 cents???"

You get direct eye contact on this question.

The only way to save yourself in this situation is to tell the kid that George's father steals from the church poor box.

That should fix loudmouth George!!

As I remember, our house was a temple of money changers during Allowance Day.

The children were as restless as natives on the verge of rising against their colonial masters.

There were times when it was more debt paying than allowance paying.

During the week, either my wife or I borrowed a bit here and there from this kid and that for movie money or when our loose change gave out.

Somewhere the kids learned about interest and we were in trouble from then on out.

Thus I advise, never fall behind.

If enough of you do—well, you know about the Social Security mess.

~

ART OF THE BIG BANDAGE

One of the best remedies I know for cuts and bruises on the five-year-old is the Big Bandage.

It has worked magic for all my squad.

When the first five-year-old draws a smattering of blood, there begins a wailing that any California Highway Patrolman would be proud to have on his car.

It could stop a speeder a mile away.

The Big Bandage, I find, is a fine pacifier. It allows the ego to overcome pain.

About 50 percent of the wailing, resulting from a skinned knee or a strawberried elbow, can be placed in the same category as Tarzan swinging through the trees giving his call.

It lets the world know what's up.

The girl has discovered, even at five years, that the reward of a Big Bandage is more lasting than a loud cry.

And it is easier on her throat and on my nerves.

I am very orderly. First the antiseptic, then the Band-Aid, which normally would suffice, except that the child must cry some more to draw attention to such a small bandage.

I decorate her for bravery by winding gauze liberally around the wound area.

As the bandage gets larger you can almost feel her pain subside.

New thoughts are occupying her mind.

"Wait 'til I show Mamma," says the patient.

I consider myself a specialist of sorts. Because I have studied her crying language.

When the child is crying full tilt and trying, at the same time, to tell you what has happened, only an expert can understand her verbal hieroglyphics.

"WAAAAAAAEEEEELLLLARMOOOOEEEAAA!"

Interpreted, this means: "I fell down and hurt my arm!"

A regular doctor would not know this. He would not know where to look and heaven knows how much blood would drip out before he found the wound!

Once I find the general area, I can work out the details.

"Where on your arm?"

"WAAAAOOOONNNNMMMYYYAAAAAHAAAND!"

"Well, let's see your hand. Where on your hand?"

"RRRRRIIIIITTTTHEEEEEERRREE!"

By bringing her hand to the light and with the aid of my reading glasses, I can spot the gaping wound.

If I really squint!

Finding the wound is the hardest part, but once I have it spotted I apply the Big Bandage.

The heart transplant surgeons may get the headlines, but I'm the cat's pajamas around here.

~

I cannot understand, no I cannot, why parents get so up-tight over a teenage party.

When they discuss the subject their faces drain of blood, their eyes reflect fear, and they tend to stutter.

Where is their faith and confidence in the young?

Why, as I type this column in my study there is a teenage party underway downstairs.

As I type this column, there is a—I said that, didn't I? There is no reason in the world for me to be nervous!

Everything is so quiet.

QUIET!!!!

Excuse me!

Ha!

They were eating doughnuts. Everything is in order as I knew it would be.

The 16-year-old's mother and I have been subtly assigned upstairs. Where we are presently crouched—I mean relaxing.

An acquaintance of mine on the California Highway Patrol told me once that they are most effective merely by being seen on the highways.

Merely a precaution, I walk through the revelers, fixed smile, eyes locked forward, ear canals wide open.

The eight-year-old is on duty as a spy, making periodic peek reports from the stairwell.

"Somebody's drinking apple cider," she reports, panting from waddling up the stairs.

"Thank you, Mata."

She rushes back down.

Back up.

"Some girl is dancing with my brother and the lamp is out by your chair!!!"

"Sweet mother of pearl!" I gasp.

My wife says, "Stop chewing your tie!"

My legs feel rubbery.

I rubber down for a walk-through.

They are dancing to the music of the Grateful Dead and the vibrations have jiggled the lamp bulb loose.

They said.

I went up to our bedroom. My wife was clinging to the headboard of our bed as it rocked.

"Merciful heavens," she gasped, "what are they doing down there?!!"

"I think they call it dancing," I said. "Calm down."

"Are the lights on?" she said.

"There's nothing to worry about," I said in my strong male voice.

"Look in the mirror," she said.

I looked. There were a series of varicolored rings diminishing in size around both eyes.

The music stopped below.

I light the filter end of my cigarette.

There is a horrible crash.

"Dear Lord," cries my wife. "What happened?"

What has happened is that our eight-year-old spy has fallen through the stair hide-away into the party.

As I type this col ... I think I mentioned this someplace!

Music is now low and slow.

No report from spy.

Am frantic!!!!

Walk down stairs and find that my spy has fallen asleep in her hidey-hole.

I think I feel faint.

~

When an offspring starts eyeing your clogs under the bed, you can feel the time passing.

It signifies a new age bracket.

It means you've fed the young'uns too well, and your wife is now the third tallest in the family.

The 16-year-old has grown well in the feet. (I had originally planned to bind them as the Chinese once did, but I decided it was too far to reach over my wife's dead body.)

I suppose it was only natural that his feet and my new shoes should find each other.

It was love at first sight.

For the first couple of times, he asked humbly, explaining that the occasions ranked higher than Queen Elizabeth's Coronation in importance to his social standing.

So off he went in my new wing-tips, polished enough to shine in the dark.

Last week do you know where I found my shoes?

Under HIS bed!

I asked if I could borrow my shoes back.

He said, "Okay."

My new shoes have led an exhausting existence this last month or so.

Learning dance steps that would never work on my feet.

And it is safe to say the shoes never clomped a maiden's tootsies, for they dance barely within shouting distance these fruggy days.

I understand that if one's partner became thirsty and left the floor to get a Coke, she'd never be missed.

"Hey, that was a tough Monkey I did. Did you catch it, Isabel?"

"Beats me, Claude, I sat out the last four dances."

"Oh, I coulda swore I saw you once."

The 16-year-old claims his dancing is easier on shoe leather than the waltz or foxtrot. His dancing is sort of a stationary stompless stomp.

When he goes out I have to polish up my old wing-tips or stay home.

With vitamins and loaded breakfast foods, the current generation of fresh ones is growing faster than pater's pocketbook.

I am beginning to notice that my sock supply is diminishing and sweaters aren't hung where I hanged them last.

It's getting downright Communistic, all this sharing of my sartorial property.

Not all, thank heavens.

The pants are still all mine!

~

◇◇

One thing about me.

When I say, "No," to the kids, I mean it!

And so I don't have the problems that most parents have.

For example, when the seven-year-old wants a game of ping pong, I say, "No."

She knows I mean it, and so she doesn't whine.

She knows it won't do any good.

So she asks, "Why?"

"Because I don't feel like it."

"When will you feel like it?"

"I have to get the meat on the barbecue."

"Whataya gonna do after that?"

"I'm going to string up the sweet peas."

"Whataya gonna do after that?"

"I have to, uh, I don't know."

"Well, do you think you'll feel like playing ping pong then?"

"I'll think about it!"

"Well, while you're thinking about it, how about a game of ping pong?"

When I originally said, "No," I meant it, but by now she has me so confused that I have a paddle dashing for the ball, trying to think about what I was trying to think about.

The 15-year-old uses a different strategy.

"Can I go to the beach?"

"No, you have to cut the lawn."

"Okay."

Too easy, I know I'm in trouble.

"Can I use the phone?"

"Sure, why do you ask?"

"I have to call up Joe's mother who is coming to pick me up."

"Oh."

"And then she'll have to call up the rest of the kids and tell them the beach party's off."

"Why can't they go?"

"Because I was going to bring the hot dogs. I don't mind for my sake, except it will sure disappoint the orphan."

When I said "No," I meant it, but who can possibly compete with an orphan?

So I had to say, "Okay."

But I got to wondering, and, just as he was going out the door with the hot dogs and bathing suit, I said, "That's noble of you kids to take along an orphan. Who is he?"

"My friend Peter, Dr. Kenney's boy. They adopted him when he was a baby."

And they wonder why I am prematurely gray.

~

THE STOMACH ACHE

Very clever, these kids.

The first three words they learn in life is, "Mommy," "Daddy," and "scheme"!

The seven-year-old likes school, but she is a female and thus has 3,486 more genes than a male to aid and abet her in the art of scheming.

When it comes to getting out of going to class.

This is amazing progress when you consider she is only seven years on this round earth.

When the notion strikes her, and this is only supposition, understand, my being only a male, she is perfectly normal up to 15 minutes before leaving for her school.

Suddenly she has a stomach ache.

"You don't have a stomach ache."

"How do you know?"

"Because you don't look like you have a stomach ache."

"Do you have my stomach?"

The trap has been sprung.

I am in it.

It was my mother's theory that we had to show pain before she believed us and it had better be in bed. Before we got up.

In fact, if we wanted to stay home from school bad enough, we had to start the pain about 4 a.m. and get her out of bed. Then she was mildly impressed.

And if we were THAT sick, we wouldn't mind taking castor oil?

My brother and I had one of the best attendance records in the history of the Kingsburg school system.

Nowadays one doesn't dare question individual motives.

Especially if she is a future liberated woman and has a liberated mother.

"All I did was wonder why she suddenly had a stomach ache just before school!"

My wife says, "Are you a doctor?"

"We've been married for 350 years—don't you know what I do for a living yet?"

"I am often confused," she says.

"Don't be crass. I'm only saying she doesn't look like a person with a stomach ache."

The seven-year-old takes her cue at this point and starts holding her stomach and quivering her lower lip.

This, of course, clinches the situation.

Like the New York Jets having a six-point lead and recovering a Buffalo Bills' fumble with only one minute left in the game.

"I'd better call the doctor, then."

"It's not that kind of stomach ache," she says.

"What in heaven's name kind of a stomach ache is it?"

"A personal one."

"Oh."

I wonder what doctors' daughters do?

Poor things.

~

◇◇

I found a substantial part of a cheese sandwich stuffed in the car's back seat ashtray.

Time and time again, Dr. Spock warned me, "Don't force a child to eat."

Yet, these are hungry times and I don't like to see food wasted.

I've not followed Spock's advice on this point, although he's been proven right.

The sandwich was in tight, stuffed with vehemence.

There was an immediate pursing of the lips on my part.

Old Indian fighters would have read this sign.

The child doctor said that, like sparrows, they'll open their mouths when hungry.

I was raised in a different kind of nest.

My father never abandoned the table until the last child had cleaned his plate.

And my mother would back him up, saying, "There's plenty of mouths that'll close without any food this day."

I heard this 358,257 times between ages six and 14. (This was kid math.)

And she was right, of course.

I haul a lot of kids around in car pool arrangements and my next time around I have a notion to line 'em all up at parade rest and hold an inquiry.

"Who ditched the cheese sandwich in the car?"

I know their reaction well enough.

"Cheese sandwich?"

"What car ashtray? Front or back? What color was it?"

Nobody squeals.

Or they'd go into a huddle and announce, "We take the Fifth!"

In my Depression days, we cleaned our plates and, to gain extra favor, wiped the plate with French bread chunks.

Well, I've learned.

When the kids were tykes, I began noticing that we had a very fat dog, a very fat cat, and some very fat goldfish.

I've learned that bribery does not work, either.

How many "horsey back rides" have I given in exchange for a clean plate?

Note my swayed back.

And, when the moon is full, my whinny.

~

"Who started this fight???" I thundered, tritely.

"He did," said the 12-year-old, traditionally.

"Meeeeeeee??" gasped the nine-year-old, typically.

"Who started the fight??"

"I wuz only—!!"

"He grabbed my Beatles autograph!!!"

"Huh?!!"

"STOP!! What does all this have to do with throwing magazines in the living room?"

"He pushed my chair in the kitchen!"

"You leaned back and touched me!!!"

"Boy! Ha! I'll bet!"

"STOP! That was an hour ago. What are you fighting about now?"

"I'm sitting here reading and he kept looking at me!!!"

"Like this! How'd you like someone to keep looking at you like this??"

"Oohhhhh, I didn't look at him like that!!!!!"

"Well, how DID you look at him??"

"Like this!"

"Well, that isn't so bad."

"It wasn't like that!!!"

"What do you mean?"

"He smiled!"

"Well, don't you like people to smile at you??"

"Not when he does it like this—!!!"

"Jeeez, can I help it if I look like that when I smile??"

"Boyyyyyyyy!!"

"Well, the best thing to do is to ignore him."

"I did, but then he kept clearing his throat!!"

"I—DID—NOT!!!"

"All right, what was that sound then??"

"I had something caught in my windpipe! Whaddya want me to do—DIE?!!"

"See??"

"Well, try not looking at each other."

"Who wants to look at HIM?"

"Enough, enough, enough!"

"It's okay with me."

"Me, too."

"There, see how pleasant life can be?"

"Daaaaaaad!!!!"

"What now?"

"He's breathing hard on purpose!"

~

Starfish are nice, but in the ocean they are nicer.

I do not relish their coming into my life.

In many, many ways, I am not ready for them.

Thursday, the six-year-old came home with one in her lunch box.

"I found it on the ground and already we like each other," she said. "See?"

"Ohhhh," I said, parentally, trying to superimpose a smile on a face horrified by the smell.

There is a psychological second in all father-child relationships when a child expects to be dominated and is ready to give in to a command.

I missed it by asking, "Is it alive?" when my years on this earth should have tipped me off that NOTHING alive smells that bad.

"Save it, save it!" she cried, and old dummy-noggin had to leave his typewriter and rush the starfish to water.

We put water in a glass baking dish (my wife put me in hot water later) and sprinkled salt in to simulate the ocean (it's a wonder I didn't stand there and make waves) and then we peered at it long and hard for signs of life.

"It's dead," I said hopefully.

"No, lookit, a bubble!"

Apparently even the dead object to domestic salt in their water, but I went to the *World Book* to ascertain how dead a starfish can be before a child is satisfied.

"Starfish have remarkable powers of regeneration," said the book, dang it. "You can cut one in half and each of the pieces will develop into a new individual."

"Let's try!" she said, jumping up and down, and I said, "Good Lord, child," and rolled my eyes and read on, but wished I hadn't.

A starfish has a colored eye at the end of each arm, but I refused to look. Lesser sights give me nightmares, and I can almost predict the form it would take—my wife pointing at me with a colored eye on the end of her finger—"You put that awful thing in my baking dish!"

At any rate, the 14-year-old, the world's most persistent humanitarian, came home from school and announced that death was relative and how would I feel lying there having people debate over whether I was alive or dead?

"Besides," he said, "I saw one of the eyes blink."

My vote said it was dead, but I was now outnumbered and besides the six-year-old had already named it "Fred" and announced that she would take it to school the next day for "Show and Tell."

The next morning there was a pre-breakfast hue and cry that "Fred" needed real ocean water.

"No wonder only one of its four eyes will open," said the 14-year-old, "and that one only stares!"

Well, a six-year-old can't get in the car and go down to the sea for water, can she? Only daddies can, right? So Daddy, in his black business suit, drove to the beach and raced back to the surf with a child's beach pail, resembling what could only be a madman who had suddenly flipped his lid and decided to drink sea water!

I drove her to school with the thing in the pail and later that day drove to school to pick her up.

She was the last to leave the building.

Alone.

In a far window the haggard face of her teacher followed her progress.

I just caught a fleeting glimpse, but on that face was an accumulation of eons of silent suffering.

Fred WAS dead.

~

I stood amid the clutter and, in round Shakespearean enunciation, said, "Will you please clean your room!?"

These are fine old Anglo-Saxon words—except for "please" which is Middle English—and to a bright elementary student, I had counted on them to convey a singular meaning impossible to miss.

"Whaddya mean, clean my room?"

I failed.

"I mean, look at those clothes on the bed post!"

"Oh, those!"

He wadded these up like an old candy wrapper and stuffed them into a drawer. He wadded them meticulously to demonstrate to me his fastidiousness.

"Okay, how about all this junk on the floor?"

He surveyed a great pile of stamps, six burned-out light bulbs, the exploded innards of a table radio, a stack of 49'er football cards, including three outdated Y.A. Tittles, a Monopoly game with the marker on Boardwalk loaded with hotels (obviously the game had ended here and was left intact as a monument to victory), a convention of marbles, one swim fin, alarm clock springs, a pile of mockingbird feathers, and a small army of monster models.

Fathers know how to hurt their sons.

"WHAT JUNK?"

How could I call stamps junk when one might turn out to be worth $1000, which he WAS going to use to buy me a new car and his mother a fur coat?

Burned-out light bulbs: Bodies on which you add arms and legs to make "men from space."

Football cards: He has already been offered an autographed photo of Batman for his three Y.A. Tittles.

Alarm clock springs: He has definite plans to put them back into alarm clocks when the need arises.

Marbles: All ready for the next game.

Radio: "I'm gonna fix it."

Mockingbird feathers: "You can throw those away."

One swim fin: He wanted to keep it "in sight" so he'd know where it was when the other one turns up.

Monster models: "They're attacking!"

Monopoly game: "I won the game—see that marker on my Boardwalk? That was his last move, boy!"

"Okay, so it's not junk," I said. "However, clean your room."

"But I gotta go to the show in an hour!"

"Look, a boy with a broken arm could clean up this mess in 5 minutes—easy."

"Aw, I bet he couldn't."

"I say he could, and fathers know!"

"In 5 minutes, with one hand? How?"

I showed him.

Did it in 4 minutes.

With one hand.

And half a brain.

~

We have a problem getting the seven-year-old to bed at night gracefully, so I said to my wife the other night, "Why don't we show her how she appears to us. Maybe it will change her attitude."

"It might work," said my wife. "What part do you want to play?"

"I'll play the seven-year-old," I said, and so when 8 o'clock rolled around that night, my wife, instead of reminding the seven-year-old that it was her bedtime, turned to me and said, "It's time you were getting to bed."

"I said, "Aaaaaaawwww, I'm not even tired!"

"It's 8 o'clock," said my wife.

"Look," I said, "how much pep I have," and I turned two somersaults on the living room floor, damaging 70 percent of my body.

"You're only seven years old and your little body needs rest," said my wife.

"Awwwwwwww, how come the boys get to stay up?" I said.

"Listen," snapped my wife, "they went to bed at 7 when they were your age. Now do as I say!"

"Can't I even see Lucy?" I sulked.

"No!"

I started to bawl.

"You just don't understand my needs," I wailed.

My wife said, "I tell you what. Go get into your nightgown and I'll read you a story!"

I gave my wife a look that asked, "Wasn't this carrying our act a little too far?" but she returned a look that said "No."

So I stamped my foot and went into the bedroom and got into my pajamas. It was the first time I can remember getting into pajamas at 8 in our 22 years of marriage.

The seven-year-old was fully dressed and enjoying it.

"Hurry up," called my wife, "or you'll have to go straight to bed."

I came back into the living room and curled up on the sofa next to my wife.

She gave me a maternal hug and straightened my nightie.

"What would you like me to read to you?" she said.

"Read me *Winnie The Pooh*," I said, clapping my hands.

"It's too late for that," she said. "I'll read you a *Just So* story."

"Maaaaaaaa," I said, "you promised last night."

So I had to sit through a whole *Winnie The Pooh*.

In the meantime the seven-year-old had gone downstairs to watch Lucy on TV.

When my wife finished, she said, "Now go wash your teeth and go to the pot."

I stomped off down the hall to the bathroom and then I went to bed where it was cold and lonely and after a time it was so quiet that I got up and put on my slippers and snuck out to see what effect our little act had on the child.

The living room was empty.

I went downstairs into the playroom. My wife and the seven-year-old were sitting on the sofa watching the Jackie Gleason show.

"Shhhhhhhh," they both said.

"We're trying to watch the show," said my wife.

"Whatta you doin' outa bed, Daaaad?" said the seven-year-old.

~

Our children, hardly out of the womb, have squirming little minds about which some people have theories.

One of which suggests that these little minds should be exercised early in life; that we should let our infants glom onto little notions and run them up little flagpoles.

The Montessori system of handling pre-anything children leans at this angle.

It has its dangers.

For one thing, I think 12 is too young for a United States president.

But because I am putty in the hands of educators I reacted benevolently when the four-year-old felt an urge to try her powers at making Cornflake Kisses last evening.

It's a simply MARVELOUS recipe.

We got it from our September issue of *Humpty Dumpty*, a child's *Ladies' Home Journal* without the advertising.

To exercise the child's mind, the theory is one must practice indulgence just short of the point of letting her stick her fingers into the electric mixer blades. (Imagine a woman president with three fingers missing. I mean, how could she salute the troops?) But let us get on with the recipe, which, by the way, makes 30 small kisses.

Practically an orgy!

Give the child two eggs and explain to her that only the whites go into the bowl.

Next give her a spoon and have her fish the yellow parts out.

Now that she understands she is not ready to separate egg whites, start all over, this time doing it yourself, and give her a little dish of ice cream to make her stop crying.

Let the child turn on the beater ("It doesn't go, Daddy!" That's because big intelligent Daddy forgot to plug it in, not having been noticed by his parents until he was almost 14), and beat the egg white until stiff.

Gradually add the child .... I mean gradually have the child add three-fourths cup of sugar.

We cut it down to a half cup, since she spilled one-fourth cup on the floor.

Next I set a box of cornflakes on the table. All the while, understand, she is chanting, "Lemme do it, lemme do it!"

Her little brain is churning for positive action. She adds two cups of flakes to the egg whites and enough on the floor to create a fine forest fire sound effect when one crosses the kitchen floor.

All this time the child is being praised.

Eventually, when she has her own home, she will spill corn-flakes on the kitchen floor, expecting to be praised, and will become neurotic and far right, politically.

Unless, of course, she weds an ex-Montessori boy.

Lastly, to complete the recipe, I bade her gently fold in a half cup of shredded coconut and a teaspoon of vanilla.

Mix half-heartedly, then spoon out dabs of goop onto a greased cookie sheet and bake for 12 minutes in a 325 degree oven.

Discourage child from accompanying kisses.

Well, I tellya, Mabel, you oughta have seen that child's eyes!

Actually, they were closed; she was asleep.

The Montessori system does not cover cleaning the kitchen mess.

~

I hugged and smacked my way through three children in the ancient past.

Of course there were sweet, gentle kisses, but for some reason they do not stick to the memory.

What I do remember is that kissing the four-year-old daughter was strongly akin with leaning my cheek against a partially melted Eskimo pie.

Mily was a particularly soggy kisser.

In fact at one time I had her kisses recorded in various categories.

For example, she gave a very fine ice cream kiss.

An osculatory dessert composed of strawberry ice cream, chocolate topping, and remnants of whipped cream.

Her milk kisses were common.

They left a sort of chalkish ring, readily recognized by other fathers at the office.

Her most indelible mark was her licorice kiss, imprinting a black tattoo containing at least three ounces of goo.

Today, you might call it cheek graffiti.

But, I think the most impressionable offering was her mush-for-breakfast peck.

Peck is perhaps on the weak side.

It might be better described as a collision with a wet custard pie.

I also remember that you took your kisses a la serendipity.

From experience I know when you tell a child, "Go wash your face before you kiss me," it takes away the spirit of it and places the kiss in a duty kind of mode.

Besides, as I recall, she would not include drying after washing.

As a result I got a wet wash rag kiss that would do credit to a car wash.

Well, as I am wont to say, an oatmeal mush kiss is better than no kiss at all.

The boys' bussing span was shorter.

The thing with boys is that you have to get in your kisses early.

They start scrunching up their faces at an early age.

The oldest, Mark, was a good hugger. As a babe he was right at home on my shoulder. He was born a Londoner, where I worked in the news business.

A beautiful baby, he made an early imprint by upchucking on my new Bond Street suit while we shopped in Selfridges.

I just grinned redly, tipped my wool cap, and said, "How-de-do."

The middle kid, Mike, had his day back in the U.S. of A.

The grandmas were always smacking him.

Grandmas get away with kissing boys longer than the parents.

"Give Gramma a kiss."

They are good huggers, too.

"Owwwwww, Gramma, I'm not a sausage!"

Going back to another time cycle, I had an aunt I'll never forget.

She was big bosomed and strong of arm.

When she enfolded me unto herself, I soon learned to take a deep breath, like pearl divers do, because I entered into uncharted territory.

I could hear her coo—things like "my sweetyums."

But her words sounded distant for I was enveloped, as it were, my lungs filling with talcum powder and eau de violet.

I am not advocating less enthusiastic hugging and kissing.

Nay, there is not enough of it these non-touching days.

Right? Right.

~

The four-year-old has a mighty powerful weapon.

She was born with a lower lip that rivals any others I have seen, and I have been the helpless victim of several in my time.

It is one of the few weapons a little girl has, although I do not believe she is fully cognizant of its effectiveness.

Like an elephant who wonders why everything moves out of his way when he becomes irked.

Time is on her side.

Not being an expert on this particular piece of anatomy, I have little defense against it.

The fact that this pouting protuberance is attached to a female may be the key to the mystery.

When the world is not spinning in her direction, her lower lip slides out like a salamander from under a rock.

It's just a guess on my part, but I think this drawing out of the lower face pulls down the lower eyelids which form sort of two dams to keep the tears back when life flows like a Montovanni string section.

The face clouds like a St. Bernard's who has just stepped in his milk.

Then we know we've got trouble, right here in River City!

Her emotional machinery is about the same as others of her species.

Who knows what can set it off?

A roller skate she left on the stairs.

And after I land and lie broken and soiled on the floor, I, perchance, might work up a fleeting scowl across my pain-wracked face and she, perchance, might interpret this as hinting disapproval!

Out slides the lower lip.

It quivers!

It affects the chin like a distant earthquake.

Then the dams break.

Sweet Land o' Goshen! What is a man to do?

But lo, I am learning.

Her lower lip makes an excellent weather vane.

I find I have about 5 seconds to make amends after it slides forth before the floodgates open above.

When I can stem the tide I feel rather powerful myself.

~

Well, it's "What did YOU do at school today?" time again and sometimes, with the six-year-old, I'm sorry I asked.

"Gregory burped!"

"He did what?"

"He burped in the cafeteria—all the boys were burping—right in front of the girls."

This is first grade sophistication, and the burping adventure is her first social event of the year.

And it saddens me.

I have lost a cherub.

But I've gained a burper.

For the past week she has been trying to burp in case it is needed to become a part of the group.

It's an "in" noise.

Even though her attempts in these early stages sound like a frog who has been asked to sing a soprano solo at the Forest Folks' Jamboree, it is a clear sign that she has discovered social sense.

And I am losing out.

She arrives home with a fist full of papers that look interesting.

I ask, academically, "Well, how was school?"

Meaning, "In what academic areas did you find yourself pursuing most diligently?"

She says, "Dennis tripped me two times!"

Or, I might inquire into which segment of her school day was most exciting, alluding to arithmetic, writing, or reading?

She says, "When Larry came into the girl's toilet by mistake!"

I remember the old days (last year) when one of the highlights of her day came when her mother or I drove to school to pick her up.

Now, it's walk or die.

Last year she loved to be read to. Now she has learned to read her first words: "a," "the," and "Vote no on Proposition 9!"

I'm kidding, but she thinks she can read now, and I am doomed to sit on the sofa, peering over her shoulder, while she reads book after book, picking out the words she recognizes.

"The—the—ah, the—the—the."

I've got the heaviest case of lead eyelids in town.

Time is cruel when you lose the only fat-cheeks left.

I must face reality, I suppose.

But if any smart-alecky first grader kid comes calling in his red wagon and sits outside and honks instead of coming to the door for her—he'll hear from me!

I may be losing a daughter, but I want to lose her with a little class.

~

It isn't easy on a father to discover that his beautiful daughter is a non-student striker, but upon sober reflection I've decided that four is a good age to get it out of her system.

Her activities originally came to my attention when she refused to take her nightly bath.

I didn't think too much of this until she began keeping her hair wet so that it would appear stringy.

But the real shocker came to her mother and me when we drove her to the Miss Muffet Nursery school and were told that her re-admission had been denied.

We were told by the dean of admissions that our daughter was a leader in a militant organization called FTSHDDDNP which stands for Freedom To Sing *Hickory Dickory Dock* During Nap Period.

Well, you could've knocked us over with an old Reagan poster.

Miss Muffet managed to keep it out of the papers, but it ended up with the whole nursery singing *We Shall Overcome*, *Hickory Dickory Dock* and going home sleepy.

This was three months ago.

Now the four-year-old is embroiled in another fracas at the school. We can tell, because she stopped taking baths again.

The way I understand it, one of the parents, who happens to be a naval recruiting officer, donated a potty to Miss Muffet's Nursery and our child, who cannot abide any form of fighting, except with her brothers, took exception to this.

Encouraged by several left-handed students, she brought her own potty to the school and set it up next to the military potty. Across the back of the potty chair she had me print "PEACE!"

Either her mother or I have to take her to the edge of the campus each morning or else she won't eat her mush at breakfast.

This current demonstration started with her making several speeches to the students during their orange juice period, then sitting on her PEACE potty the rest of the class!

Soon several other students brought their own potties, some with "DEMOCRATIC" written on the backs.

This is very humiliating to her mother and me, but what can we do?

The administration refuses to give back the military potty and the last I heard 28 students are sitting on Democratic potties or "PEACE" potties.

This includes one teacher who is sitting in sympathy with the strikers.

Several of the male youngsters have rubbed charcoal on their chins in lieu of beards.

Miss Muffet's alumnus, of course, are indignant, and I have received several nasty letters.

All I can do is to write back assuring them that they should expect this sort of thing among four-year-olds.

~

THE TWO-YEAR-OLD GIRL

I have a two-year-old female hanging around the house who is rather difficult to describe.

She's a frazzle-haired, dumpy, awkward ball with sticky fingered limbs, who covers the floor plan like a squatty vacuum cleaner, gleaning distasteful objects from underfoot and reaching them up to her reluctant catch-all—mother.

She's a cut-out doll that waddles.

She is a many-sided packaged deal with strings leading to the heart and stamped with love.

She's a crudely written poem, unintelligible, yet unimpeachable; sentimental as James Whitcomb Riley; silly as Nash; and at the same time, complex as Whitman.

She is a natural resource of ego which she mines and pumps into her guardians who use it sinfully and brazenly.

Her nose is often a running brook which she will fuss to conserve.

Her mouth is a wondrous cavern that she seldom sees, yet hand-explores and turns inside out with noise. Her tongue is a welcome mat and nothing that fits past its border is barred.

Our two-year-old is a house marcher as responsive to music as a Spanish American war veteran and their gaits are surprisingly familiar.

She is a huntress of love and her weapon is her open arms and an unsteady toddle and her aim is true and wonderfully deadly.

The two-year-old is a private showing, bursting with beauty, line color and form that we, for the life of us, cannot see in someone else's two-year-old girl.

She is a beggar, endowed with a pitiable pout and persistent one-syllable musical grunt that means, "Give me anything my heart desires."

Asleep she is Aphrodite, framed by the sides of her crib, a delicate living thing, un-erred by her own weaknesses and un-sculptured by the conflicts of becoming an entity.

She is an elixir to her grandparents, 10 times more effective than Geritol.

She is an elucidator of one's raison d'etre, a harbinger of hope, and a human enigma that needs no solving.

Our girl is a bottomless receptacle of worthless prose from the adults—high-pitched, teeny-weeny gibberish, twisted words which will take years to rake away.

She has an extraordinarily powerful vocabulary of two words —"Mommy" and "Daddy."

She has an operatic cry of Wagnerian proportions and little reservoirs under her eyelids for holding excess tears.

She is dead weight around the neck of her older brothers.

She is a student of the pratfall and I hope the repeated pounding does not reflect on the shape of her derriere in later years.

She is 90 percent eyes and 10 percent grab.

That's our two-year-old girl.

DEAR DAUGHTER:

Your letter says by words and feelings that you are lonely and miserable at the university and that your classes are overwhelming you. It is, on the face of it, difficult to believe, because the campus is so beautiful and you are so fortunate to be there.

But, I do believe it. In my memory, you have company. If it is any consolation, I went through the same fears and doubts that you now feel.

It was a long time ago, but when I visited your tiny room in that great expanse of campus and thumbed through those seemingly endless books you are charged to read, it reached deep into my memory.

I was 18 when I went away to school, an awkward kid who had never really been away from home.

Your grandfather had died when I was a high school sophomore and your Gramma took over the family.

When it came time to go away, we packed the old Studebaker and drove to the school. Then she went away, leaving me in a totally foreign environment.

I was short of funds; I had no friends; I was thrust into large classes that ran 100 or more students.

The main goal was to endure, to survive the whole exciting, unpleasant, grown-up, strange situation. To quit and go home was unthinkable.

I was pledged to a good fraternity, and briefly moved into the house, but it was a zoo of loud music, fast drinking, and eternal distractions. I decided to find more studious climes.

But I wasn't happy with the move—to a boarding house, run by a stiff-lipped woman who was forced to take in students, but didn't like them.

I had a tiny room on the third floor and the stairs squeaked like snitches. It was cold and isolated, a place to brood and pine of home.

It was understood that I would work. Within a week I had found a job as bus boy and dishwasher in a restaurant.

I remember the overwhelming constant odor of used food, mixed with cigarette butts. My clothes smelled of tuna fish and stale potato salad.

I fell into a forlorn routine of studying after classes to 4 p.m., walking downtown to the restaurant and working until 9 p.m., then returning to my little room to study to midnight.

I tried to improve my hour arrangement by unloading box-cars at the Southern Pacific freight docks. The hours were right, but the body reached for the bed when I returned to my room.

I wanted to go home; I wanted to break away, perhaps to another college, another land, but none of these would solve my frustrations. I felt trapped.

Everyone else seemed to be well adjusted, contented, cool. It was not true, of course, but it seemed so because I could only think of my own problems.

Every minute of my time seemed to be devoted to working on class assignments and reading or working outside.

I would often do homework for one class while listening to a lecture in another.

I worked in an ice rink, in a candy kitchen, checking rail-road refrigerator cars for bums before they were iced, in a cannery, and as a fish salesman.

Gradually, I made friends. It dawned on me that those around me were real people who were faced with similar problems.

The dean of students at my college spotted my hangdog appearance and walked me around the campus one after-noon, spouting philosophical encouragements into my ear. It helped.

I began to see substance in my classes and sometimes my seemingly insufferable academic strugglings paid off with glowing comments written on the margins of my papers by my professors.

After a time, life seemed lighter and more purposeful. When I figured I finally had my act together, I joined Delta Theta Omega and started living it up a bit. I began to think I would survive.

You have it easier financially, which I believe is necessary to obtain the most from your studies, but this is not to say that you don't have the same fears and loneliness and doubts as I had.

Be patient. You will soon begin to recognize and feel inwardly proud of your metal and perseverance.

You will be using these attributes, for life will present you with a series of like tests.

This is not your first.

You will remember the backpack trips where you fell from a switchback and said you couldn't go on; where you said you couldn't make certain high mountain passes.

Just remember. You made them all.

~

WAR IS A TERRIBLE THING

War is such a terrible thing.

It's so noisy.

Especially at the front—which, in this case, is in the back.

I mean in the backyard.

The conflict has been churning up the quiet for a half hour now and, like most wars, this has no cause celebre.

A series of senseless shooting, killing, and reincarnations.

"Pow! Pow! I got you."

"Come on, George, you're dead, you gotta fall down!"

It's an appalling spectacle, but we ace war correspondents become callous to these things.

I am also callous to miracles.

George counts to 25 and arises anew, like a self-patching inner tube.

I also witness quirks of clemency by the enemy.

George is allowed to retrieve his rifle, which he dramatically flung aside in the throes of sloughing off his mortal coil.

The enemy barks off another count of 10 so that George can fade away to fight again.

War is hell.

Especially when you consider the cause of this one.

It was caused by the eight-year-old.

Pre-war, an hour ago, the combatants were moping around the house kicking chair legs, like a scene from *Marty*.

The 11-year-old said, "Whatta you want to do, George?"

George said, "I don't know, whatta you wanna do?"

The eight-year-old, who wasn't asked anything, said, "Let's have a war."

He's mature for his age. Wants to go into government.

His idea goes over with lung-top enthusiasm and incurs the wrath of the territorial governor (my wife) who semaphores frantically with her apron not to wake the baby, who is too young to be subjected to the rigors of war.

Although, in a few years, she'll probably be allowed to be Florence Nightingale, or Clara Barton.

War is very complicated in our neighborhood because of a mobilization problem.

There are three 11-year-olds and one eight-year-old. And the 11-year-olds, who are developing strong sheep tendencies, find it psychologically disturbing to let an eight-year-old into their herd.

However, there is an overriding factor which opens the corral gate to him.

The eight-year-old is heavy on ordnance.

He has a couple of plastic rifles, a six-gun, a plastic mortar, and a piece of polished manzanita which Mother Nature blessed with the semblance of a carbine.

He uses this balance of power like a chubby-cheeked Caesar.

The 11-year-old suggests the two other 11-year-olds take a vote to determine who wants to be on the eight-year-old's side, and then closes his eyes so he won't know who voted against him.

His ego still has growing pains.

He opens his eyes to see that Joe has enlisted with the eight-year-old. The manzanita stick is Joe's favorite weapon.

Combat around our yard is practically 100 percent semantics.

The major din consists of "Pow! I got you, Kent, Joe, Mark," or whomever is gotten. Identification is fatal.

"Blam!" indicates the unleashing of heavier artillery, and a hit in this case is more disintegrating.

"FAROOM!" is more atomic in nature and, at least in the mind of the Faroomer, gloriously splatters his opponent over several acres.

This makes resurrection more of a bother.

Occasionally, two swashbucklers tie on their "Pow! I got you."

In this situation both emerge from their respective outposts and hold loud debates in no man's land, which places a strain on hostilities, because it leaves only two generals in action.

Therefore, it has been mutually understood that when a tie occurs, the "pows!" are regarded as misses.

As I say, we calloused ace war correspondents are hardened to these battles; but once in a while we catch a new angle—like the other afternoon.

Above the rattle of gunfire and stunted roar of the bombings and the hideous screams of the temporary dying, I heard the shrill voice of the eight-year-old cut across the battlefield in a general appeal.

"Kings! Kings! I gotta go to the toilet!"

~

"WATCH!!"

The three-and-three-fourths-year-old is entering a stage in her life which is dominated by the word "Watch!"

On a dining room chair she stands poised, like Tarzan on a cliff showing off to Jane.

But instead of the Tarzan yodel (of which I was neighborhood champ, if I do say so myself), she hollers, "Watch!"

"Watch, Dad!"

"Watch, Momma!"

"Watch, Dog (her cat)!"

"Watch me jump!"

If Momma screams, "My lord, she'll kill herself!" it only heightens the drama.

According to Dr. Spock, the human computer of childhood, who, I am certain, will be a shoo-in for the presidency when the current mass of his chicks and chums across the nation reach voting age—the three-year-old has discovered her motor.

The whatchamacallit that drives her coordination.

A full carton of milk is poised over her small glass.

"Watch, Dad!"

"Watch, Momma!"

"Watch, everybody!"

"My lord," screams the wife—but it is too late!

"Watch me," I say, "I'm going to get the mop!"

This little kitten is racing her motor these days, and the book says we must show appreciation to keep her id from rusting.

In the back of the station wagon she has completed a masterpiece in crayon art.

"Look, Dad!"

"Look, Momma!"

"Oh Lord, watch the road; you'll kill us all!" shouts the woman beside me.

What the little one is doing, of course, is trying out her ego.

It's what we all do throughout life, only in subtler forms with hundreds of variations.

I'm soft as a ripe peach to her demands.

I could go through life raising three-year-olds, except that, kiddo, they don't stay three.

After a year of bliss they turn four.

Four is an ancient word meaning "monster."

But at three we are a captive audience and everything she does is a command performance.

Is this not so, Doc Spock?

After the seventh time she performs a summersault we are stuck for expletives, for the doctor did not put an eighth in his instruction to parents.

"Wonderful, that's cute, grand, fine, oh, ahuh," and "um-mmm," just about completes my repertoire for this age level.

Especially when I have to come out of the shower each time to catch the encore.

And I have learned that one must not falter or become inattentive during this period.

I am reading the evening *Bugle* on the couch and the three-year-old is drawn to her full jumping height on the back, above me.

"Watch, Dad!"

"Watch, Momma!"

"Good lord, watch out!" wails my wifely protector.

"OOOOMMMMMFFFF!!"

~

Well, it has finally happened.

The five-year-old has left hearth and home for kindergarten.

Kindergarten. That's a German word meaning "get 'em away from father while they are still educable."

The last child under my influence has flung herself into the grasp of the Great Society.

They have lured her away with orange juice, sweet talk, and fast boys.

The first day she returned home she could hardly contain herself over "a new friend."

"He had orange juice with me and slept with me but we haven't talked yet."

I've wrung my hands so much, they're peeling!

Only a week in this hallowed hall and she's already been reorganized by other females.

"Every girl in my class has a Barbie doll except me!"

This is her first lesson in group behavior.

Two weeks ago life was beautiful.

A scroungy caterpillar scrunching up her arm made the day for her, made her feel rich with material possession.

Now I am the object of scorn for not providing her with the conforming wherewithal of every other little robot girl in town.

Her look, I'll never forget. It accused me of being a Madison Avenue drop-out.

Even a week before kindergarten began she was inspected like something just off an assembly line.

She looked all right to me.

Oh, there was a mosquito bite on her left knee, but by the time inspection day was over she had been peered at by an earologist, checked by an eyeologist, shot by a pediatrician, evaluated by a psychiatrist, and for all I know made out her last will and testament!

I'll be frank.

I think this is an underhanded governmental way of ferreting out future lady astronauts.

Ah, 'tis a sad week.

It hasn't been spelled flat out to me yet, but it has been insinuated that my role from now on is to provide a home base, keep a good supply of Band-Aids on hand, and lay low.

Or is it lie low?

It's a hard fact of life for a father to take.

Before kindergarten began, the five-year-old doted on my every word.

I was her DeGaulle.

Now her *World Almanac* is her teacher. My image faded like last night's sunset.

Even more omnipotent is the principal who could not possibly be an ordinary mortal, according to the description rendered by the five-year-old.

He probably emerges out of paste pots and walks 6 inches above the ground.

I once saw a sad movie about the place where old elephants went to die.

Funny I should remember that now.

~

THE STAR OF BABBLE

There is utter rejoicing under our roofed menagerie tonight.

The 11-year-old returned home from school shouting that a red star had been placed on the classroom blackboard in his honor.

I know the boy has great perspicacity, acres of acumen, not to mention freckles around the nose, and that it was only a matter of time before the academician of 5-B recognized his genius.

"A star in your honor! Bless my soul," I said, rocking back on my heels. "What on earth for?" (as if I didn't know, he being a chip off the ol' block).

"For not talking out of turn in class for one whole day!"

"Oh."

He continued, "I was the only one in class to get a star." Only the manner in which he said it actually consumed nine minutes.

Oh well. This is a victory of sorts, and Dr. Benjamin Spock, the Horatio Alger of child rearing, is firm about the value of praising the child for all successes.

So we shook his hand.

Spock says it keeps his id lubricated.

I can well imagine his bedraggled teacher considered the star a major victory.

So we are rejoicing and making up words of praise—when we can get a word in edgewise. A boy can get awfully pent up when he spends a whole day not talking out of turn.

We are wondering if he'd go for the star system at home.

When he's talking in the other room I think someone forgot to turn off the radio.

"If no one's listening to that thing, turn it off!" I yell.

He has the continuity of a Lucky Strike tobacco auctioneer.

Sometimes we don't understand him because his words jam up before he can get them out of his mouth.

Some actors spend years and hard cash learning to project their voices.

"There are girls in my class who can whisper and the teacher doesn't even hear 'em," he said. "I whisper and his glasses fall off sometimes!"

In his last year's class they had a short period called "Show and Tell" where the children brought flora and fauna to class and talked about them briefly before the class.

Word got around to me that once the 11-year-old warmed up to his subject, the teacher had to raise her hand for 3 minutes before he gave her permission to take the floor and tell him to sit down.

I see a future for him in the diplomatic corps—in one of those shacks like on the 38th Parallel in Korea where our talkers and their talkers go to talk instead of the two sides fighting.

Eventually I see this kind of thing taking the place of war so talkers will be in high demand.

The boy should fit right in, but he should stay clear of Russian opponents.

He'd spot the Russian Star in the room and stop talking, and the consequences might be serious.

~

My life is too filled with words and bills and rushing about from Point A to Point L to notice the growing of a child.

In my mind there is a vague, wishful hope that the child will wait.

Fed by smiles and shrieks and girlie mannerisms and routine hugs and a face partly camouflaged by Popsicle red and play yard brown.

A little girl goes unspotlighted, except for her demands for a peeled apple, a book read at bedtime, a push on the swing, a chest in which to bury her head in time of tears.

But it's been said you lose a child a little every day, and this seems to be true.

To know, you have to pause and unfasten your mind.

Watch as casually as smoke uncurling from a pipe, to see the slow unfolding.

Like a new marigold blossom opening in the morning sun.

The bottle of Jergen's lotion on her dresser. How can she make hands softer than they are now?

The handkerchief of her own. I noticed that. Why, before her mother always held an extra one of mine to evoke a "blow."

The hardening of her play dough on a corner shelf.

Building blocks half hidden by sophisticated dolls.

Where Captain Kangaroo's likeness used to fill a portion of her bulletin board, The Banana Splits now reign.

And then there will come a time when she starts snapping her fingers in time to rock music and saying, "Yeah, baby."

Or she'll tramp through the house chanting, "I'm the first kid on my block with a broken heart!"

"What's a broken heart?" I'll ask.

"It's a song."

"Oh."

You lose a child a little every day.

And, reflecting these changes, would I want it to be different?

In her room, I see her bed is half-made.

Two pieces of underwear had almost made it into a dresser drawer.

And nobody gave the order!

It is sad, in a way, to see a child slowly move off of her island and absorb the ways of others.

The signs are there.

I should recognize this when she says so frequently lately, "I did it all by my very self."

It gives one a fading sensation.

And then she will be 15 while I am about my busy ways.

So I think what I shall do is stay home from that meeting tonight and devote the evening to more important matters.

Like horsey-back rides.

~

COME INTO MY TENT!!!

It's tent city afternoon in our living room.

"DON'T step there, you might squish one of the kids," shrieked my wife.

"It's all right, I'm over here," muffled the five-year-old. "I'm over here."

"Where are your friends?"

"They're where I guess Dad was about to step!"

There is scant room for adults; the living room is under "canvas."

When I was in coveralls I had to be satisfied with a card table and a bed sheet.

Today kids have grander ideas.

There are blankets and bedspreads all over the big room.

Benches, chairs, and card tables and the back of the sofa keep the sprawling tents up, one connected with the other.

All anchored with piles of books, zig-zagged in such a hurried way that if the *History of The Roman Empire* fell, it would pull off *Advise and Consent* and unbalance the *World Books*, and the whole city would collapse.

The scene looks like a Bedouin Winchester Mansion.

I am seeing the third child indoor tent architect in my fatherhood. The current five-year-old is reaping the skills acquired along the way. Under my tutelage, of course.

There is no way of telling how many inhabitants are crawling around on all fours underneath all this material.

I only see sliding humps where the blankets slide over their backs, as they move about playing out their fantasies.

"Come on in my tent, Daaad!"

"Aw, I'm too big!"

"Come on in!!"

Well, I don't have to be asked five times.

An architect should inspect his own instructions.

It is dim inside.

Then dark under the thicker blankets.

My knees hurt.

I immediately become THE MONSTER!!!!!!!

"Yeee, he's after us!!!!!!!!!"

"YEEEEERRRRRROOO!!!!!!," I growl.

And HISSSSSSS!!!

The screams are deafening!!

The whole neighborhood must be enclosed here.

I feel the power.

Suddenly the monster experiences total deflation.

When I put the full weight of my right hand on a peanut butter and jam sandwich.

The monster's left knee tips over a glass of milk on the rug.

"MAMA, DADDY TIPPED OVER THE MILK!!!!"

"Perfidy!!" I grumbled. I hear thunder approaching.

"Honestly—a grown man!!"

I hump up and immediately feel the *History of The Roman Empire* on my back and *Advise and Consent* consenting!!

Tent City was falling!!

Kids are bawling (sounds like about seven) all over the place!!

Well to heck with them.

I am buried under blankets—feel like Hamlet's ghost with a fist full of peanut butter and jam.

I think I'll just stay here and bawl!!!!

The sky is dropping silver wetness, and I am trying to write.

The rain is not getting me, but the sniffler is!

She is working studiously in a corner with her crayons and color book, but there is a cold-factory in her head which is producing on a wartime basis.

And I cannot hold a thought for more than 12 seconds.

Which is the average time between sniffs.

"Sniff."

Eight, nine, 10, 11, 12—.

"Sniff."

Eight, nine, 10, 11, 12—.

"Sniff."

None of the other offspring were so persistent nor so deadly in their timing.

She begins around January 10th and dries up about the time the first daffodils bloom.

To say that it drives me mad would be going too far, for I am still allowed to walk the streets. (However, to lessen suspicion, I usually remove my Napoleon hat before leaving the house.)

So we won't use the tag, "mad."

I think "dingie" will do nicely.

"Could you please stop that sniffling, I'm trying to work!"

"Sure, Daaad."

Eight, nine, 10, 11, 12—.

"Sniff."

11, 12—.

"Sniff."

15 seconds.

"Sniff, sniff."

The double sniff is a make-up for being late on the previous one.

My wife says to me, "Don't complain; at least we know where she is."

At the neighbors' the sniff is fainter.

There is no indication of a cold.

But, if you ask me, there is some indication of sadism.

"USE YOUR HANDKERCHIEF!"

"I haven't one."

"Well, get one!"

"Where?"

"Ask your mother."

"Sniff."

"Mother's down shopping."

11, 12—.

"Sniff."

15 seconds.

"Sniff, sniff."

"Why don't you go downstairs and watch TV?"

"Cause the guys are watching football, and they said they can't hear the quarterback with me there."

"There, your mother is back now; how about a visit with her?"

"Before she left, she said go see you—before she screamed!"

There is no way out.

"I am it."

Eight, nine, 10, 11, 12—.

"Sniff."

~

It is not always necessary to create sophisticated presentations to provide high adventure for your children.

Simple outings oh, such as "sleeping" overnight in the backyard, lulled to sleep by father's chattering teeth, can simply thrill an eight-year-old.

Even though the house is a scant dozen yards away, their tiny imaginations soar.

"WHASSAT, DAAAD?!!! Sounded like a wild animal!!!"

"It's just me—I was hungry for my salami, but bit into my flashlight!!!!"

Another time she was frightened by what sounded like a wild cat scream!!

I had to tell her, in pain, not to panic—it was only my vertebrae grating against lounge springs.

"Is THAT ALL? Good night, Dad."

The eight-year-old daughter chose the hammock on which she laid her down sleeping bag.

I got the chaise lounge, under blankets.

Camping equipment: a flashlight, now damaged by my molar indentations, a rusty sword, and a baseball bat to ward off assorted boogie personages.

My motivating drive was, "Well, what is one night roughing it out back for the delight of a child?"

Except that I didn't count on the day part.

She went to bed around 7 o'clock, so it was embarrassing lying out there under blankets with my night cap on in broad daylight!

With my bare feet sticking out the end.

Especially when a couple of strange ladies appeared in the yard for some promised flowers. They circled the flower beds casting frantic stares my way. (The eight-year-old scrunched in her bag like a bewildered turtle.)

I nodded my head stiffly, like a Japanese movable garden statue, and started to say "How-de-do" but the cotton ball of my night cap flipped over and lodged in my mouth!

My wife explained something briefly, that I was her husband.

She said it in a tone I am sure conveyed to the ladies that I was serving time out here.

Night fell.

And so did I out onto the wet lawn.

It is certainly amazing how soaked a night lawn can get.

Isn't it?! Or don't you know?!

The drawback of such an adventure is truly that children miss all the thrills and adventure.

The eight-year-old fell fast asleep at 8:30 p.m.

Leaving me to stare wide-eyed into the night, wondering when the bogies were planning their attack.

Midnight.

My first trauma occurred when I heard a strange noise, and peered wide-eyed into the night to make out two whitish objects seemingly perched near the end of my bed.

Here I use the word "bed" in the sense of self-torture equipment used to atone for one's sins.

I waved my sword in the air preparing to strike when I recognized my feet wagging futility trying to keep warm.

1 a.m. I know why Elliot the cat sleeps all day long ... because he's a sex fiend all night! I don't know who he was after, but Elliot and some brazen fence walker collided in a passionate winging that had all the earmarks of a hard rock band playing a Chinese opera, with feeling!!!

Sweet Howling Apes!!!

3 a.m. Up to put the eight-year-old back in bed.

4 a.m. Experienced the thrill of discovering a fat snail on the big toe of my right foot! Now I think I know how Humphrey Bogart felt on the Jungle Queen. Except he didn't scream like a woman!!!

5 a.m. The eight-year-old awakened, sparkling with energy, and looked across to see a strange man with varicolored circles around his eyes, locked in a fixed stare.

There was a reason for this.

At that moment another lounge spring was trying to perform a kidney incision on my backside.

"Hi Dad," she said, stretching, "WOW, this was fun."

"Wasn't it?" I said, feeling for blood. "We must do it more often!!"

~

LITTLE GIRLS' ART OF CRYING

Little girls have built-in cries.

Their cries are as accurate as a marksman's arrow, mostly striking the heart.

As different from the boys' as the mating call of a moose is from a robin's spring song, yet more effective.

Little boys have more of a Falstaffian wail. And, sometimes, as a variation, a moan, like a freight train blowing its whistle in a long tunnel.

Little girls come from different factories.

Their cries are carefully worked out presentations—moving concerts filled with synchronized emotions which paralyze the air.

A teary downpour may be motivated by the most unpredictable circumstances.

Like a scowl, a perfectly logical refusal (like a doughnut before supper); a suggestion that she wear her red dress instead of her blue one.

Or, a request not to walk on her father's stomach when sent to awaken him of a morning.

The mechanics of a little girl's cry are pre-set.

Her face becomes a moving front of darkening clouds.

The lips quiver. Then they quaver like the flank of a horse attempting to startle off flies.

And you know it is about to rain.

She mobilizes her tears into plopping silver pearls that dance briefly on the rims of her eyes, and then tell their sad tales as they slide down her flushed cheeks.

Not bad for openers.

On occasion, a dampish tone poem of woe.

She holds the mortgage and she is preparing to foreclose.

Little girls sense their power early, and all the troops assembled to guard a parent's point of view panic, break ranks, and run like cowards.

Timing. Oh, do they have timing, Charlie!

They have a rheostat regulating the magnitude of their cries.

When quivering lips won't light the lamp above the male's head, up goes the rheostat.

The eyelids become like weakening dikes from which a new flood of tears flow; the shoulders shake like San Francisco in 1906.

In seconds they can project their miseries with the devastating effectiveness of a William Jennings Bryan oration.

Their faces embody the tragic spirit of Heidi and Little Orphan Annie and a hint of Sarah Bernhardt, all rolled up in one.

Against such awesome odds, I am immediately reduced to Herman the Jellyfish.

Adrenalized guilt is programmed into the male system since Adam, and I am on Submission Boulevard.

That's the way it was meant to be.

~

SCHOOL BUSES ARE FOR CATCHING

Catching a school bus of a morn asks for punctuality on the part of the catchee especially in the summer when it's loafing time.

The six-year-old who answers to Mily put on a grumble the other night concerning having to go to bed early so she could rise bright and shiny to catch the summer school bus.

Well, after her mother rendered her prone, opened a window a crack, and soothed the sheet near her chin, I came in, sat on the edge of her bed and said, "Tellya what I'm gonna do."

"What?" she said.

"Just for you, I am going to make some special arrangements. Starting Thursday, instead of you going to the bus stop, I shall have the bus driver come especially for you.

"And not in his usual everyday pants and shirt and tie.

"He will be wearing purple pants with gold stripes down the legs, a belt of sparkling diamonds, and an orange shirt with jelly bean buttons and cuffs with licorice strips.

"His shoes will be pink and soft with loop the loop toes.

"And each shoe will have a music box attached, one for melody and the other for harmony, and they will play, *'For she's a jolly good girlee, that no one can deny!!'*

"His hat, oh his hat will be something, all right!

"Tall, like a drum major's, I think silver in color with a little door in the center, and out of that door will pop a red bird on a crazy spring and it shall call out, 'Good morning,' I believe!"

"WOW, SUPER FAR OUT!!!!," she shouted, her eyes round like a Walter Keene painting.

"The driver will shake you gently by the shoulder, then, take one step backwards when you awake and salute in time with the music on his shoes.

"Then he will leave, and return to the door of the bus while you breakfast on popcorn and ice cream, ala upside down cake.

"Wait—that's not all!

"As the driver returns to the bus he will tell two of his kangaroos to kick out a red carpet, thick as spring grass from the bus door to ours.

"If you wish, I will have the bus repainted. How about with strawberry jam? Fine, with a giant sunflower sprouting from the radiator.

"When you have finished breakfast, and excused yourself, I have arranged to have your old friend the Cat in the Hat escort you to the bus to the tune of *Ain't She Sweet?* as played on the banjo by me, then a stewardess in a tutu will escort you to your bus seat.

"Now, your seat will have your name in gold plate. Your seat will also have special springs so you can bounce on it and special side rollers so you can squirm.

"I am having The Banana Splits band flown out from Omaha, and they will set up a fountain and serve chocolate sundaes to you and your friends on the way to school.

"And for entertainment there will be a parade down the bus aisle with bunnies pulling a coach coated with sapphires, a frog brass band, a white mice drill team, two miniature poodles doing the Can-Can and a quartet of owls singing, *'Who!'*"

"Come on, Dad, really?!!"

"Well I'd like to know why not????"

"Daaaaaad."

"What?"

"Tomorrow night will you tell me another fairy tale?"

~

CHAPTER 6

DEAR SCOUTMASTER

A MEMORY OF SCOUTING DAYS

Dear Scoutmaster:

Please excuse the dirty writing paper. I am under my house digging a fallout shelter with all my might. Time is short, I fear. I have a boy in your troop who is working on his atomic energy merit badge upstairs, which is why I am under the house, 7 feet down so far and digging.

My boy is the one with the Einstein haircut and the Seaborg grin.

I am under the impression that he is taking this altogether too seriously, and I cannot understand why you would include such a merit badge in the Boy Scouts.

It is upsetting enough to live in a world filled with paranoid leaders fiddling around with atomic diplomacy.

When I was a tenderfoot, we helped lacy old ladies cross the street. They were less explosive.

I wish you would send a nuclear specialist over to the house and check this boy's progress.

There is something strange going on.

Sir, our house is shaking.

We hear rumblings in the night.

My wife has to sleep in an asbestos nightgown.

And I found 14 beta particles in my peanut butter sandwich this morning.

Mushrooms are growing out of the kitchen faucets.

And Goldie, the Dog, resembles an irked porcupine.

I am giving this note to my dog to deliver, as I understand he knows where you live, having often visited your front lawn.

We fear that our boy has progressed beyond the requirements needed for this merit badge.

We suspected this when he asked that we re-wallpaper his room for his birthday—with LEAD!

His model nuclear reactor has a curious hum to it. Once, just to check, I rented a Geiger counter. I really don't understand how it works, but when it played *Nola*, I figured something was amiss.

There are other signs that tell us he has gone beyond the point of no return.

For example, the milk in my Post Toasties glows.

At breakfast, he mumbled something about critical mass and I said, "Beg your pardon?" and he said, "I said mass," and I said, "You can't, you are not ordained!"

Little humor there.

But at dinner last night, he casually asked me how many atomic bombs Russia claims. I said, "Oh, I don't know, maybe 500," and I could see him counting his fingers under the table.

Then, early one morning, I could hear him practicing countdowns in his room!

That's when I got up and began digging this fallout shelter under the house.

I must get back to work now, my shovel has started to reproduce itself.

~

Dear Scoutmaster:

We, I should say, my boy, has completed his merit badge requirement in astronomy, thank heavens.

I said "we" because I've been looking at so much sky lately, I think I know how Charles Lindbergh felt by the time he reached Paris.

If you'll excuse the expression, this project has been a pain in the neck. Last week when he finished identifying his final constellation, I tried to look down to congratulate him and couldn't.

My neck has become permanently affixed in the general direction of Taurus the Bull.

My, aren't there a lot of stars, though?

The Boy Scout handbook says that the naked eye is supposed to see more than 6,000 stars. I guess my eyes aren't naked enough. I could only count 4,785.

We were handicapped by a lack of a telescope. I wrote a kindly letter to the Lick Observatory people, asking them if we could borrow their glass on a clear night.

They wrote back and said their glass was bolted to the floor and couldn't be moved. Otherwise they would have been glad to let us use it.

A Boy Scout never gives up, however, so my boy told me to keep looking skyward in case he missed something. A stiff neck is not so bad outdoors, but in the house I soon became bored. I know every crack and cobweb on our ceilings and am on speaking terms with three spiders.

The boy had some difficulty in understanding the moon principle behind ocean tides, so I said, "Come with me to the beach, and I will show you."

High tide came in sooner than I expected and we spent an hour spread-eagle against the face of the cliff.

"What does this demonstrate?" he said, hugging the cliff with water to his knees.

I said, "How to save your life!!"

He said, "This wasn't one of the requirements."

I understand that some of the Scouts have been having problems with the star names. I can sympathize with them, sir, they are all in Latin, or Greek, or Arabic.

Perhaps at your next troop committee meeting you might bring up the possibility of giving them more practical names —like Durante, Hope, Crosby, Gabor, Monroe, Lollobrigida—well maybe you better skip that one—Nabors, and so forth.

Another difficulty these days is locating the constellations. Several times we spotted what we thought was the handle to the Big Dipper, only to discover that it was a 747 heading for Japan.

But persistence has overcome and I think he is ready.

His next step is to take his test from the astronomy merit badge counselor. I understand that Mr. Ugla is a specialist on Mars and a stickler for accuracy.

This might take a while. I tried to contact him yesterday but his wife said he is far away for some special surgery.

She said he was under the kitchen sink the other day fixing the drain and bent his antennae.

Yours Truly,

~

COOKING—BROMO SELTZER

Dear Scoutmaster:

I—

Excuse me, I had to dash for a Bromo Seltzer.

There.

I am not feeling well at all. But I figured I had better write you about my boy's attempt to earn his cookin—

Excuse me!

Whew! Almost didn't make it.

About this cooking merit badge.

He has been practicing at home and his mother and I feel that this should not be encouraged. They should confine their cooking to the woods. Hic!

For the past three days he has insisted on cooking the meals.

In the backyard; more specifically, in my garden. I am the only one in our block with smoked marigolds!

Excuse me, my Alky is fizzing.

We are fading fast, with still tonight's supper to go.

For breakfast yesterday morning he served liver and rhubarb.

And a slice of German chocolate cake on top of our mush.

His mother and I have been mixing our Alka Seltzer in a canning kettle.

For lunch he served tacos stuffed with lemon Jello with a dehydrated prune juice sauce.

Dessert was baked Alaska with frozen tomato paste ice cream.

Excuse me, please.

Had to run down for another case of Pepto-Bismol.

We never did identify the vegetable. It was grayish and supple and in various shapes. Neither of us dared ask what it was, even though the boy challenged us with, "Bet you don't know what that is!"

I looked out the window and noticed my Caster bean plant was missing. About a pint of blood drained from my head until I remembered that I had yanked it out the day before.

Tonight he is preparing stew, his one-pot meal, and I am becoming rather frantic because I haven't seen the dog all day.

The poor thing has been barking at us. Our stomachs have been growling so much I do believe he thinks there are a couple of angry dogs around which he can't see.

His mother has tried to make suggestions, such as, "We don't make dumplings with raspberry cake mix," but he is very independent.

Actually the raspberry dumplings weren't so bad. It was the broiled garden snails that caused us to collide in the hall on the way to the bathroom.

We wrestled for a while on the floor for firsties, and I won.

But my wife and I are nonetheless happy to make certain sacrifices for the Boy Scouts of America.

It has thrown us into the spotlight in a way.

Our doctor has informed us that we are the first known people in medical history to become addicted to Tums.

~

Dear Scoutmaster:

It may seem to you that I spend most of my time in bed, which isn't true.

Between my boy's Scouting activities I am well enough to move about normally.

Today I am writing to you to verify that my boy made his 10-mile hike. I was there, which is essentially why I am in bed with my feet in slings.

They are two flaming nubs.

My doctor has called in several scientists. He said he has never seen toes fused together!

When we returned from our 12-miler (he insisted on the extra 2 miles in case his pedometer was off), my wife said she noticed something different about me.

There was. I was on all fours.

She said she didn't mean that! She went for her tape measure and sure enough, I am now 3 inches shorter. For the first time she said she could see the bald spot on top of my head.

Actually the "bald" spot is where the hair scraped off when I fell.

He yelled "canyon" and I thought he said "companion," although while lying on my back at the bottom I reasoned, "Why would one say companion when one's father was poised in mid-air over a chasm?"

He could have yelled "tablespoon" or "auto mechanic."

Sir, I know Boy Scouting is for rugged kids, but level with me. Isn't your organization secretly training future commandos?

He took a route that would have made Lewis look questioningly at Clark.

Everything was a challenge to him. We challenged a great deal of poison oak and I am covered with so much Calamine that I am sure I could make the next issue of *National Geographic* as an Australian aborigine.

I am one horrendous itch!

My eyes are so puffed that as I write this letter it's like squinting through the gun slits of a Loomis armored truck.

But I'll say one thing. The boy was meticulous in preparing for the hike.

I told him we wouldn't need a 5-gallon can of water for such a short excursion, but he rose up to full stature and said, "A Scout is prepared, sir!"

On MY back a Scout is prepared! I don't like to be always complaining, but staggering 10 miles in a stooped position with 5 gallons of water on one's back tends to leave one with a Neanderthal stance.

It bothers my wife when my arms swing in FRONT!

It also affected my vision. My eyeballs are still frozen in the "up" position.

I must close now. I see the doctor has come with the snake bite serum.

The boy yelled, "Snake!!" and I thought he said, "Wake!"

Sincerely,

~

Dear Scoutmaster:

Forgive my squiggly penmanship, sir, but it is cold in the backyard where I am bedded down.

The last time we spoke you wondered when the boy would complete his requirement for his dog care merit badge.

You and me both.

The dog is in my bed.

In the name of Boy Scouting, I am willing to humor my boy, but I am growing weary of playing dog's best friend.

There should be a merit badge on father care.

The doghouse is too small and I feel like the Red Baron sleeping on top.

I asked my boy why he didn't have the dog sleep in HIS bed and he said he originally intended to but he didn't have an electric blanket and Charlie balked.

And I had just gotten to sleep on top of the doghouse last night when the boy woke me up and said Charlie didn't like the heat level so I had to go up and change it from 6 to 3.

Not only have I had to give up my bed, but I am expected to take over his dogly duties.

I am expected to bark several times a night so the neighbors won't get used to the quiet in the dog's absence and louse up his routine.

Also during the past week I have been challenged by three cats, two of which won.

Charlie is not a particularly easy dog to work with for this merit badge.

He is a member of the SPCA—the ACLU of the canine world—and he knows his rights.

One time I merely mentioned that it was time for him to get shot for distemper. He called the police. When they came he rolled over on his back and pointed at me.

Charlie is also claiming that I insulted him yesterday.

One of the merit badge requirements requires the description of the characteristics of 10 breeds of dogs.

"That's going to take some study," said my boy.

"On the contrary," I said. "It's easy. Just write down 'Charlie.'"

To get even he gave me three of his fleas.

I usually speak of the dog in a soto voice because Charlie senses when he is slighted and holds grudges.

On two occasions he has pushed the dryer in front of the back bathroom door trapping me inside and then howled to drown out my call for help.

My concern now is that Charlie is showing signs of adapting to his new environment. He likes my bed. I can hear him snoring from here.

Like you said the other day, you have to be a good sport to be a father of a Boy Scout.

I agree, but there are limits.

My boy has taught Charlie to whistle.

The other afternoon when he and the neighbor dogs were sitting around on the front lawn, Charlie whistled for me and I had to go out and shake hands all around.

I refused to "roll over," however.

The lawn was wet.

~

HELP! THERE'S A BOA IN MY BED!

Dear Scoutmaster:

I know you have problems enough with all the kids in your troop, and so as a parent I am sorry to have to bother you. But sir, I am in bad trouble again.

My boy is working on his reptile study merit badge, which is fine with me, except that at this moment there is a boa in my bed.

If my typing seems light, it's because I am hitting the keys very daintily: I do not want to make the snake crotchety.

I'll bet you are scratching your head and wondering why there is a boa in my bed and why I am in bed with it. Well, sir, I don't blame you one whit.

Let me assure you I am not lying around eating bonbons. I have been in bed for three days because this boa is wrapped around my leg.

In case you are curious, it is my left leg.

My reason for writing you is that perhaps at your next district Scouters meeting, if the agenda is not too full, you might bring the subject up on the chance that there might be someone in the room who has removed boa constrictors from other legs and can throw a hint my way.

I would have called the SPCA right at the beginning, but my boy said the boa is only on loan to him for his project and goes to the Parker boy after my boy is finished.

I happened to know that Mrs. Parker becomes hysterical over the sight of a worm. I can't help but wonder how she will react to this 12-foot snake.

My boy made a bed for the boa in our pet dog's box because, unfortunately, the dog has no further need for it.

But the boa took a shine to my wife and me instead and slid into our bed.

My wife is still in the attic.

The boy has been taking her food. I can't leave the bed with this boa on my left leg, and he figures he has to do a good turn every day anyway.

Part of the requirements for this merit badge is to observe a reptile for a month.

I have tried to stimulate his observations with questions such as, "Why do you think the boa wrapped himself around my leg?"

He has deduced that the snake thinks my leg is a tree limb.

I went one step further and asked why the snake would think that?

"Probably because you are shaking like a leaf," he said, writing it down.

Even when paralyzed with fear I can recognize a bit of drollery.

But there is a time for sober reflection, and getting serious for a moment I am uneasy about the future. Even though I have been in bed three days, I am very tired.

I have trouble getting to sleep at nights.

This is partly due to the fact that I must sleep spread-eagle, for my boy warned me that the boa was probably waiting to get my feet together.

I think it has something to do with swallowing.

My boy has a good mind when it comes to boa constrictors.

I hope you will give my letter some thought.

You know where to find me.

Sincerely,

~

HER GOOD TURNS ARE KILLING ME

Dear Girl Scout Leader,

Excuse the motel stationery, but it must do while I am hiding here.

I am writing you to inquire about the Girl Scouts' good deed system.

I have an ex-Brownie going into GS this September and already she has this good deed bug.

Couldn't you have waited? I feel that I am a prime candidate for the funny farm.

I am hiding in the motel because it just became too much. Last night she brought me a bottle of beer from the refrigerator.

"Here, Dad, my good deed," she said.

"Thankya dear," I said, taking a long pull at the bottle.

It was CERTO!

I am the only man in town with a preserved stomach.

The night before she put Three-In-One oil on my electric toothbrush.

My teeth keep slipping when I chew, and it hasn't improved my smile. My wife says I look like a card shark.

I am not quick to alarm.

I told her there was no need to continue her daily good deeds until she became a Girl Scout, but she insists on practicing.

The other morning when she couldn't come up with an idea, she washed the morning newspaper.

Those inconveniences could be overlooked. They didn't involve danger.

But I first became alarmed when I casually complained that the spring in my reclining chair had weakened.

She talked her brothers into secretly replacing it with the only substitute they could find handy: the garage door spring.

When I stretched back the other morning with my soggy newspaper, it flung me.

Ma'am, when I say flung, I mean you can still see the spread-eagle outline of my body where I went through the opposite wall.

The doctor at the hospital said it was actually better to hurt all over than in just one place.

On dull days the girl concentrates on my pencils.

She has sharpened them so often I have to hold the eraser to write.

Two weeks ago she came up with, "A safe home is a happy home."

This good turn took the form of removing the upstairs handrail to "sand away slivers." And she forgot to put it right back.

I grabbed for it that night about 2 a.m., and for a few happy seconds, I flew.

Ma'am, I never was good at night flying.

The ambulance driver said later it was the first time he had ever seen an unconscious man flapping his arms.

It has been like this for a month. I am a vigorous man, given to climbing mountains, hugging women, and lifting the side of our VW while my wife changes a tire.

I suppose it's psychological, but after three weeks of her insisting that she help me from the supper table to the sofa, my hands are trembling, and I have become irregular.

The way I feel now, I couldn't open the screen door of a rest home.

This morning when I awoke at the motel, I shuddered, wondering, "Will she find me?"

Will you write to my girl and then write me at Jock's Cigar Store, which has a bulletin board? I will pass by in disguise in two days.

Forgive my penmanship; I am nearly blind.

I complained about weak lighting in the house, so she put a flash bulb in my reading lamp!

Now, even the night is white!

~

THE HOME REPAIRER

Dear Scoutmaster:

Just a note to report my boy's progress on his home repair merit badge project.

You must excuse my awkward penmanship, for I am back in traction again, with only one arm free.

It's kinda funny, the way it happened.

Ha! Ha!

The boy needed four screws for a screen door hinge and borrowed the screws that held our living room floor-to-ceiling bookcase to the wall.

At the time I was under that bookcase. Reading an essay he had written on home safety.

He didn't let it just fall on me, mind you.

I have to admit he yelled, "LOOK OUT!" as he removed the last screw.

This gave me a choice.

"Look out" can be interpreted as follows:

1. Look out the window.

2. Look out, something heavy is falling.

I chose to look out the window!

And lost.

My boy wanted me to ask you if the work he did on me before the ambulance arrived could be counted for his first aid requirement.

I understand the screen door is fixed.

One minor problem keeps cropping up. He used garage door hinges and my wife says it takes three people to open it.

She said that the cat got caught on the in-swing yesterday and the door threw it against the far kitchen wall so hard you now can hang a coat on each eyeball!

I feel relatively safe here in the hospital and, except for a severe cold, I am doing fine.

The cold stems from the boy's wanting to help save his mother extra steps in the kitchen.

He got fooling around with the freezer and somehow combined it mechanically with the washing machine.

Our spinach comes out washed and clean, all right, but frozen shorts are murder to wear the first hour or two!

Well, like I was telling the nurse, you can't expect perfection every time.

And I must say, some of his home repair failures have been spectacular.

He repaired the light switch in our bedroom and now every time you turn it "on," the toilet flushes!

He is rather proud of this, but I had to tell him it wouldn't be acceptable toward his merit badge.

And it has become a nuisance, really, having to flush the john when we want the bedroom light on.

But he has had his successes, too.

We had a kitchen table chair with a weak leg.

He amputated it.

Like he predicted, it eliminated the wobble.

Before the bookcase incident I had been out of the hospital two whole weeks, having recovered from a dented head.

Three legs are all right on a chair if you keep concentrating on it.

You must sit there and repeat, "It only has three legs, it only has three legs!"

The reason I fell is that someone came in and asked why the chair had three legs.

It broke my concentration and WHAM!

The boy has three more repair jobs to do to complete the merit badge.

It has been arranged that I go to a rest home until he finishes. Will write you from there.

Sincerely,

~

CHAPTER 7

MAN OF THE HOUSE

HOW SUPERMARKETS MAKE MONEY

Most everybody knows that supermarkets barely eke out a profit from budget-minded housewives.

Where they make their millions is from the husband shopper. Ask any young gray-haired housewife.

When the doll of the house gives me a list and a pat out the front door, I have a smile on my face similar to that of Alec Guiness in *Lavender Hill Mob*.

Sort of a grin—most of which is held inside. Because a supermarket is my Disneyland.

It's a place where husbands can give vent to belated childhood desires and at the same time scowl like a bored adult male.

The list I am given is perfunctorily filled, mostly items pulled from shelves under signs marked: "As Advertised."

Now I am free! Free to roam the canyons of color and temptation.

Let the labels weaken my resistance. Let the succulent product photos reduce me to a salivic sucker.

I am the man who supports the packaging experts.

Take dill pickles. I don't necessarily like dill pickles. Seldom eat them.

At home there are four jars on back shelves of various brands, their tops thick with dust.

But on the label they are profoundly delicious and just last week I paid something like 45 cents for a grand jar of "Polish Icebergs."

Who could resist a label like that? Not I.

I could plainly see that the contents were dill pickles, and actually they looked like any other dill pickles, but here was new adventure. I like Polish people and I have always been fascinated with icebergs.

Freud would have somersaulted with joy right in the aisle to see me reach for that jar and drop it in the basket.

My mouth watered all the way home. I opened the jar and chomped into one and it tasted like a dill pickle.

I buy National Broadcasting Company crackers because I still think they are made by Huntley and Brinkley's mothers.

I have several packages of Japanese Bean Threads the use of which I haven't the foggiest idea.

Zucchini juice repels me so violently that I once bought a can.

And as the winter months approach, latent squirrel tendencies emerge, and I am the guy who cleans out the 10-cent discard basket filled with cans of Danish Sweetbreads that fell under the wheels of the delivery truck or Labrador Beets returned by the Salvation Army from last Christmas' food pile.

I recently bought three bars of Dove Soap, even though we haven't a dove to our name, but the words are poetic and soothing when sounded out slowly.

Pico Pico Hot Sauce has colors on the label which go well in our kitchen.

We husbands are free agents in a supermarket. We don't repent until we pass through the checkout stands.

~

I didn't get biscuits with my eggs the other morning.

My wife quietly explained why.

"There's a mockingbird in the oven," she said.

I said, "Oh," and asked someone to please pass the salt.

At our house we've had pet caterpillars on the curtains, white mice behind the TV set, a St. Bernard loose in the living room, and once an owl in the fireplace—and I wasn't about to become hysterical because there was a mockingbird in the oven.

I could surmise, however, by the facial expressions around the breakfast table that I was expected to ask "why-the-mockingbird-was-in-the-oven."

So I did, and my wife said, "Dear, after the boys found the tiny thing in the yard last night and phoned you, we decided we'd better check with the Switger boy who keeps birds and ..."

"What was wrong with my advice?" I cut in. "What's wrong with feeding it worms like any red-blooded mother mockingbird would do? What's wrong with returning it to its nest?"

"Probably nothing," said my wife in a tone of voice that would do justice to a United Nations mediator, "but the Switger boy said to feed it gruel and not to return it to its nest. He said once it was handled by a human the mother would reject it."

The Switger boy also suggested it be placed in the oven with the door open where it now squatted—every peep challenging my position as head of the family, raiser of children, admired consultant on mockingbirds.

Ever since my 10-year-old asked me how he might perk up his sluggish goldfish, and I suggested adding a slug of Old Crow to the tank, my prestige as a naturalist has suffered.

But I showed not the slightest trace of hurt dignity. I kept it bottled up inside until I reached the office. Then I called a prominent Santa Cruz bird bander and watcher of birds.

"Nuts," he said. "I've handled all sorts of baby birds and returned them, and watched the mother feed them."

That restored my ego, but I got cocky and asked for the mockingbird's scientific name to flaunt around the house as chief naturalist again.

He said it was *Mimus polyglottos*. I couldn't begin to pronounce it so I dropped the idea.

For further backing I called a Watsonville area bird watcher.

She said a mother bird will never touch its baby once it was handled by a human. I almost told her what the Santa Cruz expert had said, but decided it might only get the bird watchers fighting, writing letters to the editor, or worse yet, start a rash of mockingbirdnapping to see who was right.

I started calling other bird people I knew, trying to build up a predominance of opinion on my side. One party was still flushed from being called a name by another who called him after talking to me.

To put an end to this vacillation I put in a call to the University of California ornithology department.

Dr. Ned Johnson, assistant curator of the bird museum, came to the phone and listened to my story.

He said, "Rejection of infant birds after they have been handled by humans is an individual matter. Some mother birds will, some won't."

I considered this a rather cowardly answer and suspected that somebody from Santa Cruz County had gotten to him first.

However, I was happy to accept a draw on the matter.

During our conversation Dr. Johnson said that baby birds could be fed mashed-up dog food, and I immediately relayed this to my wife at home.

An hour later she phoned back and said the mockingbird had accepted the dog food, but now the puppy was in the oven, too.

"What shall I do?" she asked, frantically.

"Call the Switger boy," I said.

THE HORSE IN ME

You won't find my name among the horsey set, but I could qualify.

I am highly horsey.

Veddy, veddy.

Not as a rider, mind, but as ridee, or as one who is ridden.

I am presently in servitude to the three-year-old, a very accomplished horsewoman, and by accomplished I mean she accomplishes getting me down on all fours when she is of a mood for a cantor around the living room rug.

When she tires of me, I suppose I will be put to pasture until the grandchildren reach riding age, but if you will excuse a bit of braggadocio, I am presently at my blue ribbon prime.

I stand about seven hands high; I am shod, but don't use shoes where they count.

I am registered (Republican), and I have a rather prominent mane, mainly because haircuts are $2.25.

I do my best work at a slow parade walk and am unique in that I giggle when the three-year-old digs her heels into my ribs.

Which tickles. Not many horses giggle.

There are several tricks I perform that most of today's horses cannot do.

For example, I can reach back with my right front leg to steady my rider and I can also talk.

I can say, "Leggo my hair! No, I won't go out on the front sidewalk! My knees are killing me!"

As horses go, I am up there in years, but on the other hand I am still feeling my oats.

I may have been a mite more frisky under the 11-year-old, when he was a living room equestrian, and I bucked upon request, but lady riders are more gentle and less demanding and they are inclined to hug their horse if he does a good job.

I prefer lady riders.

They understand when a horse says his knees hurt.

The management and feeding of father horses are very important if there is any feeling at all in the stable.

They should be kept lean. They should be allowed to make hay every once in a while—with other male horses, of course.

They should receive back rubs by the stable girl (known colloquially as wife) following a strenuous ride. And they must never be loaned out to the neighborhood children. They should not be over-ridden.

That is, I think about four times around the living room rug is a good substantial ride.

But not having compared trail notes with other father horses, I do not know the status quo on this matter.

Maybe there is a place for a Horseyback Club, or a Fathers' All-Fours Society.

We could meet every Wednesday night and compare blood lines and have neighing contests.

And perhaps a horse show or two.

Father horses are not given the credit they deserve.

Ask any father horse.

~

Well, the colored eggs are tucked away in the backyard, and I am ready to hippity-hop back to bed.

For no respectable bunny would be caught out at this hour with dew on his slippers.

While searching for hidey-holes I came across three eggs from last Easter.

The odd number brought back dark memories, for as I recall it, one young party found less eggs than the other young party, resulting in the affluent party being clobbered on his Humpty Dumpty by the less affluent party.

A bunny's life on Easter morning is not an easy one, let me tell you, even though the layer of eggs, according to ancient mythology, possesses mysterious powers.

I use up 89 percent of my mysterious powers just getting out of bed ahead of the kids.

One Easter, what was left of my mysterious powers ran out behind the greenhouse and I fell asleep against a tree.

There was a time, when the children were tinier, when my wife suggested I rent a bunny costume to make the experience more realistic.

I quickly told her about my Great Uncle Harry who tried this.

Uncle Harry, according to the family historian, possessed a dramatic bent, and actually hopped along his course of egg-planting in a slight crouch.

The children never saw him leap around like this, but his wife did, and it embarrassed her, so one Easter he rented a bunny suit to justify his strange habit.

Uncle Harry's neighbor raised vegetables for a living, and on this early, gray dawn, he happened to peer out his window and saw this giant rabbit hopping about near his cabbages.

The gardener flung open his bedroom window, his eyes big as eggs over easy.

Uncle Harry called out from his bunny suit, "Heh, heh, good morning, George, I'm, heh, heh, hiding Easter eggs."

The neighbor disappeared for a second, returned, and yelled, "A likely story!" and put a load of buckshot in Uncle Harry's fluffy bunny tail.

So I don't wear a bunny suit.

Only a rather bunny expression on my face.

I go forth alone, and at this hour of the morning, only the snails are abroad.

Over the years I have made observations.

You are probably not aware that snails slink over the grassy blades during the night, laughing their stupid little heads off because the grass tickles their bellies.

It's a wonder they don't wake up the entire neighborhood.

And although I have only a token mental force working at this hour, I have wondered what snails must think, suddenly coming on a colored Easter egg.

Some, I dare say, leave their shells, dazzled by the color, and never find their way back!

Ah, yes, don't we all!

When all my eggs are cleverly laid (at 28 eggs I don't have to apologize to anybody) I shake the dew off my tail before entering the house and head for bed.

My wife (Mrs. Rabbit), who originally pushed me awake and out, gives me a benign look (similar to that of a Scoutmaster presenting merit badges) and mumbles from her covers, "You're through, that's nice. Eggs symbolize the beginning, you know?"

How well I know they symbolize the beginning.

Beginning Monday we're going to begin eating hard-boiled eggs and we won't finish until the Fourth of July!

~

MIDNIGHT SANDWICH

The lights glow low. There is quiet in the castle. All are abed but me. Now is the time. I am proceeding toward the kitchen, my bare feet feeling the sumptuousness of the living room rug.

There is a deep stirring within me—an overwhelming urge to build a sandwich.

I am aware that the short journey is fraught with perilous mental obstacles.

They are attacking now, like meteorites: "You're overweight already! Won't sleep. Your body needs a break from food. Cholesterol!"

I falter. My steps almost stop.

Then.

I break through this zone of doubt. Free! I have passed the point of no return and enter the kitchen.

Lateness of hour; the mental scolding; the feeling of guilt— all these are necessary prerequisites to the grandeur of a midnight sandwich.

This kitchen is the only one in the neighborhood that is lighted. It shines like a beacon, heralding my gastronomical debauchery.

A midnight sandwich calls for wild abandonment.

I open the bread drawer and fish for two firm pieces of brown. This is a plus. Healthier.

They must be sturdy, for the duty they will perform will be Herculean.

Rubbing my hands with glee, now, I fling open the fridge.

I throw a left jab into the far reaches of gleaming white enamel and sniggle a square of Limburger, exiled there by the rest of the family.

"Outa sight." It's a former expression of joy. Ah, there's a packet of pickle and pimiento meat loaf.

I take it out and put it on standby.

I spot a hunk of hamburger meat loaf and worry it out between juice bottles.

Tomatoes, sliced; a mite juicy, but we'll see.

What's this? Leftover refried beans! La, they might help cement the tomatoes together!

To the cupboards! To the cupboards!

I flip down a can of corned beef. It twirls and I catch it behind my back like a show-off baton twirler.

The material is assembled. The architect steps forward.

"Ta-daaaa!"

I happen to be a Prometheus when it comes to sandwiches. Where's the Tabasco?

On one slice of brown goes Nucoa and a schmeer of Sandwich Spread, then lettuce.

I let a light spring rain of Tabasco run down the dales of the lettuce.

Excitement mounts, and I feel the need for music and dash into the living room, clicking my heels en route.

Stravinsky; must have Stravinsky, because my sandwich is an experiment in dissonance.

Back to the kitchen. Now the meat loaf is added; now the Limburger, on pimiento, on onion, on Dancer, on Blitzen—

More Tabasco! Stravinsky's brass and tympani rise in a glorious crescendo.

Ah, glory.

Now my attention turns to the second slice of bread.

Horseradish! How in the purple world did I forget the horseradish?

If this thing is built right, dear reader, you can catch fire biting down through the bread, feel a slight breather passing through the refried beans, then reel from the sear of Tabasco as you hit the meat.

Ready on the right. Ready on the left.

Carefully I slap the two sides together.

Like a cymbal crash!

The twain has met.

AND IT IS AMAZONIAN!!

Oh, Frank Lloyd Wright, wherever you are—eat your heart out.

(Trumpets fanfare, please.)

To the table.

When the occasion calls, and this is one of those occasions, I can open my jaws like a boa constrictor.

It is not a pleasant sight.

So, if you will please excuse me—.

~

MY APPLE RECIPE

All right, everybody, into the kitchen!

You, with the long hair, gettaway from the Mixmaster.

Tonight, I should like to introduce a fine dessert recipe featuring the apple—handed down, ear to ear, in my family, as far back as Aunt Eve.

What she could do with an apple, you wouldn't believe.

So. Take four large tart apples. This might be difficult to do unless you have a private apple tree, because fruit nowadays is picked in the blossom stage and shipped to a storage house to await tasteless maturing.

Anyway, procure four apples, and if you don't want to do this, go up on the roof and sing hymns.

It is best to chill the apples in an ice box, or, if you happen to live in the 20th century, use your refrigerator. Leave them there for a half hour and while you're waiting trim your toenails.

I never seem to find the time until my wife screams, "Will you please not walk across the hardwood floor barefoot when you come to bed. You sound like a werewolf!"

Peel apples. When they are neck-id, dip them several times in a solution of lemon juice and water.

This preserves their color.

Core the apples, or, if you are handy with a .22, this makes a nice clean hole and provides a bit of sport to break up the day. A note of WARNING! Do not fire the gun in the kitchen if you have a cake in the oven.

For the love of Pete!

Also important is what you wear. You'll notice I am wearing my mauve sweatshirt and orange socks. It not only helps to light a dull kitchen but gives me the feeling that George Bernard Shaw would have liked me this way.

Now, simmer the apples in a sauce composed of the following ingredients: three-fourths cup of sugar; two cups of water (preferably from the Pedernales River); the grated rinds of one orange; five tablespoons of apple jelly; and two teaspoons of orange flower water.

Alas, you may have trouble finding flower water. I bought mine in Paris, at a little market which sold flower water. I have never used it since, but it leaves one feeling mighty secure.

If a personage comes up to me and says, "You wouldn't happen to have flower water, would you?" I can smirk and breathe out, *"Mai oui!"*

Simmer the apples in this syrup until tender. Remove them (whilst singing *Apple Blossom Time* in a rather deep, Wagnerian basso) and, if you wish, continue cooking the syrup until it becomes thick, and use for sauce.

You can serve it hot or cold. I like it warm.

Pour the syrup over the apples (ever alert to hold little finger of pouring hand aloof from the others) and squirt a slug of whipped cream on top. Top this with a tidy glob of jelly.

This is it, unless you want to garnish the serving plates with $5 bills, twisted to resemble bay leaves.

Those who swallow theirs provide much levity for those who don't.

And I'm all for laughs.

~

Forty-five percent of all emergencies, in the world or at home, which affect my life, occur while I am in the bathroom.

While the percentage may vary with other people, I have put this down as one of my serious burdens, for it is my nature to panic, even when there is nothing in particular to panic about.

I am one who must leap to the fore when trouble brews, whether it be at the side of the radio or in between two arguing kids.

And a bathroom is no place from which one should leap!

World War II began when I was ensconced in such a sanctorium.

This may seem neither here nor there, except that people are forever reminiscing and asking, especially at social gatherings, "Where were you when the Japanese bombed Pearl Harbor?"

"In the bathroom," I answer. There are tight little smiles and the subject is always changed.

I was there when Louis knocked out Schmeling and when Truman recalled MacArthur.

It is not necessarily the momentous event that has turned me prematurely gray; it is someone in the house calling out, "Dear God, Truman smalvet ergothur!!!"

The rest is muffled and there I am, not knowing whether Mr. Truman had died or hit someone with his cane!

One of my hobbies is struggling for dignity.

It has so many enemies.

One of them is a piercing scream by the five-year-old, reserved for when I am indisposed.

I rush half-dressed through several rooms, frantically ticking off the pressure points in the human body to stop bleeding, only to suddenly find myself amid a gaggle of giggling girls.

"What happened?"

"Betty tickled me."

What are you going to say to THAT, standing there the way you are, awkwardly holding my pants up?

If ever the piano is going to fall through the floor—on the cat under the house—it will be while I am in the bathroom.

Noises seem to amplify; voices become more intense.

A sonic boom is a dead ringer for my wife falling down the stairs.

A family crisis is apt to reach its peak while I am helpless.

I should be oriented after 21 years, but my wife often greets unexpected old friends at the door in a manner more apropos to being pinched on the subway.

"OOOOOOOOHHHHHHHHHHH!!"

Once I had just settled in a hot bath when this Tarzan-like cry broke loose.

I rushed out in 6 feet of skin with still an inch of water clinging to my body to find Aunt Helen frozen motionless in her furs!

She still thinks I'm kind of a nudist nut.

As the result of all this, I approach the bathroom today with nervous apprehension.

It is not conducive to one's regularity to be on pins and needles.

~

"You've a good chest structure for a man your age," said the spa instructor, sizing me up for an exercise program. I thanked him, but didn't go into why this is. It didn't seem to fit the scene.

My chest is expansive because I have been the balloon fellow in the family through three kids.

I am still known as ol' power lungs. Enough air mass has moved from my lungs to constitute a respectable north wind.

When the kids were given birthday parties, and they seemed to have them every third month, they wanted the party room festooned with balloons.

They had what I called the Roseland Ballroom on New Year's Eve complex.

For some reason blowing up these rubber balls was considered "Dad's job." Mothers bringing their kids to the party also brought balloons for me to inflate for THEIR kids' parties a week later.

I am naturally a jumpy person. I think it came from my mother who used to jump when the house furnace clicked on.

Balloons only aggravated my sensitivity. From experience, I knew that one out of every five was manufactured with hidden thin spots which would rupture during the blowing stage.

Which one would it be, pray tell?

"POW!!!"

That one?

Balloon blowing is like an ink blot test. It reveals the inner weaknesses and one or two outer ones.

My face contorts; my eyes cross. Long suppressed anxieties spring to the surface.

I remember that one of them was that if a balloon busted during inflation, so would I.

I used to close my eyes when the kids watched. I did not want them to see my eyeballs frozen in fear.

Now, it can be told. I am a balloon coward.

I would no more blow a balloon to its full capacity than I would change a light switch blindfolded.

Each puff brings me closer to pent-up panic.

The kids used to sense this and cry, "More, more, Daaaaad, just a little bit more!"

"Noumanug!" I would protest.

If I opened my eyes, I would see only a great yellow surface: a bomb waiting for just the right stress—meaning the next puff.

"One more puff, Daaaaad. Just one!"

It was like a chant from a great chorus.

"POW!"

To this day I have very unusual toes.

They turn up at the ends.

~

Like I predicted several pregnant weeks ago, my wife and I agreed on names for our overdue addition and—Zingo!

Likewise predicted, the baby began exerting its impatience at 3 a.m. while the sun was still leering at bikini-clad damsels basking on Black Sea sands.

We had carefully worked out two plans for B-day.

Plan A: Call our friend across town to pick up the two boys; then drive the wife to the hospital, c-a-r-e-f-u-l-l-y avoiding that manhole bump on Bay Street.

Plan B: Panic.

I eventually adopted A-and-one-half.

My wife quietly awoke me at 3 a.m. I say quietly, because when I go off to sleep I become "set" like a mousetrap.

For instance, there was the night my wife sat up in bed and said rather loudly, "Myrna Loy's on the roof." I don't recall now if it was what she said or what she said loudly that sent me running downstairs and out on the front lawn.

I do remember standing out there in the cold trying to think what she had tried to tell me. On the very good possibility that I had misunderstood her announcement, I rhymed several words with "Loy," like "hoy," "ploy," "coy," and "boy on the roof."

I ran back upstairs and checked the boys' rooms, but both were in their beds; so I retired, glad to forget the whole thing.

The next morning when my wife went out to get the paper, she found a slipper on the lawn.

"Whatever were you doing on the front lawn last night?" she finally asked over coffee.

"You said Myrna Loy was on the roof," I answered evenly.

"Was she there?" said my wife in a tone reserved for our eight-year-old.

"No," I snipped from behind the sports section, "but then, I only checked one side of the house." There the matter dropped.

So the other night she shook me quietly and said in a near whisper, "I think it's time to go." The words were gentle, but they had a fiercely exciting penetration to them.

I got up, squinted into the darkness, "carrumped" into the closet door, and stood there wondering what one wore when taking one's wife to the hospital to have a baby.

My wife reminded me to please hurry and make the phone call, so I went down and dialed, and when I heard the phone lift at the other end I said, "The time has come."

This made the cook at the all-night restaurant very nervous and he asked what the big idea was. At that hour in the morning, I shouldn't have tried to explain—especially when he had just placed seven eggs on the griddle.

But our conversation ended amiably, and now I wish I had gotten his name because he was the first person to offer congratulations. I mean I think it would have been nice to at least send him a birth announcement.

And actually I hated to hang up, because he had a rather interesting theory about most bright children being born between 3 and 7 a.m.—something to do with the oscillation of the earth's axis with respect to the sun.

But my wife seemed anxious. So I got through to our friend and she arrived in a wide-awake dither and got the boys.

We made it to Sisters Hospital just fine, and several *Catholic Digests* later I was informed I had eight pounds' worth of girl, 19 inches long, with dark eyebrows and a built-in cry.

It was 6:30 a.m. and lead gray outside, and the mist over the waterfront was beginning to lift like a curtain on a new play. There was a quiet newness about everything.

Through the Venetian blinds in an adjacent wing, the sisters in their billowing white uniforms were visible kneeling at their morning Mass.

Someone came in and asked me for the baby's name and I told her Mily Elaine.

And as one of the sisters observed later, "Sounds a little like Hialeah, but as long as she's a winner I guess it's all right."

~

DON'T HONK FOR MY KID

This boy came up to the front of the house yesterday afternoon and yelled out for the six-year-old.

That did it!

That cut it right there and then!

No kid is going to call on my daughter and stand out front and honk.

I went out, and with ice in my voice, said, "If you are referring to my daughter, please come inside and do it properly."

He scuffed his shoes for a minute on the driveway and followed me inside.

I invited him to sit on the sofa, then proceeded to my king-size chair, lighted my pipe and, taking my time (I had to think), blew a cloud of smoke toward the ceiling, like I've seen fathers do on the TV family series.

He sat watching the ball of smoke rise and wagged his legs.

My own daughter, hardly off her mother's breast, and now this!

"Do you have a date?" I said, dreading the question.

"I don't like dates."

(My God, I thought, he's one of those swingers.)

"You don't like dates?"

"My Mom gave me one once and I didn't like it."

"I don't mean that kind of date," I said, sternly.

"Oh, you mean, like today is Thursday?"

"I mean, what are intentions, young man?"

"What's in-ten-shun?"

If there's anything I can't stand, it's a smart-alecky kid.

Since the moment the doctor came into the waiting room and told me, "It's a girl," I knew I was in for trouble.

Boys I am used to, but how do you raise a girl?

If I have told my wife once, I've told her 100 times, "We've got a girl on our hands. Have you told her about boys yet?"

"She has two brothers. Brothers are boys."

"I mean about boys. About life. Choosing the right husband!"

"Don't be silly."

"Okay, you'll rue the day when suddenly some boy notices her."

"How long have you known my daughter?" I said suspiciously to the kid.

(The father is always the last one to know.)

He said, "She's in my first grade class."

"I see. Well, how long have you two been going steady?"

(It happens to girls all the time, these permissive days.)

"What's steady?"

(Nor do they have any respect for elders.)

I said, "Never mind. The fact is that you've come calling on my daughter. Why?"

(Let him weasel out of this one!)

He said, "I wanna play."

"PLAY!!"

"She said she has two swings and a fort and to come over and play."

"Oh."

(Whew!!)

~

WALTER MITTY, FIXIT MAN

When I am not breaking things around the house, I am Mr. Fixit.

Aided by a touch of Walter Mitty lapses.

Fearless, brave, clean, and reverent, often perceived facing zingy odds!

For example when I unclog a drain I am urged on by the trapped men in the mine, desperately gasping for air, their very lives dependent on my steady hands guiding the plumbers' helper, oh so carefully into the toilet opening and jamming it with all my might!

IT UNCLOGS! Faintly I can hear cries of relief—some calling out my name!!!

I am considered by some (well, the seven-year-old) to be a flawless stud finder for affixing hooks to hang pictures for my wife.

A sound foundation in music is required here by tapping the wall to locate the stud. A G-flat must be heard as the hammer hits it.

I must find it quickly for there are two men and a woman below me hanging by their fingertips on the cliff face, thousands of feet above the canyon floor. Their strength is fading; they cry to me to hurry.

I tap feverishly! There! G-flat. The stud! I hammered the nail and attached the mountain climbing rescue equipment just in time, and saved their lives while I was at it.

While I was in the basement relighting the water heater, I lay on my back fiddling with the regulator and began shouting in my mind, "All right commander, start the countdown. Get yourself and the men off the moon. When you get back tell my family I loved them all!!!!!!!" A lady astronaut kneels down and kisses me with fervor!!

I also had occasion to work with a screwdriver; the screw being driven home is the one that will save the submarine crew!

One slip and we all drown!!

"There, I think I've got 'er!!!!"

Swelling CHEERS from the crew!

When I change a light bulb I draw a crowd.

Being safety conscious, I turn off all power in the house.

The seven-year-old is watching The Banana Splits and the tube goes blank.

The 15-year-old suddenly finds his wood burning iron turning cold.

The horrible cacophony from the 18-year-old's stereo dies like it was stabbed! In the kitchen my wife's electric mixer mixes no more.

In this wondrous silence I am working.

They line up behind me, like four mad Donald Ducks!

But bit by bit they are awed into silence by the pure beauty of my twirling hand.

My hands are now those of a surgeon working deftly and quickly in the socket.

Done, I am slumped exhausted, waiting for the avalanche of praises.

"WHYJA TURN OFF ALL THE POWER TO FIX A DINKY LIGHT BULB???"

What I hear, however, is, "THE ENGINES ARE RESTARTING! WE WILL NOT CRASH AFTER ALL!"

~

I don't expect to attain the subtle class that the lady of the house reaches with her soups. They are like opening movements of pre-dissonant symphonies.

On the other hand, I can turn out a Breughelian pot that will inspire the drawing of a sleeved arm across a sated mouth and a Viking-like growl of fulfillment.

I have made fancy soups to exact recipes, but they only feed my ego.

What feeds my soul are soups rising out of an urge on the wild side and progressing unguided as a rudderless ship in a thrashing, heaving sea.

A case in point is the one launched last night. I was passing through the kitchen to sustain my squatter's rights and academically threw some chicken backs and wing tips roosting in the fridge, into a pot of water, to brew some stock.

Also automatically, I crunched in a dried bay leaf. Lo, that was the catalysis. The smooth crispness of the leaf and the pungent pleasure from the snapping released me from thought of other duties.

It was 9 p.m., no time to start making soup, but I cannot make soup by the clock. As the bay leaf was releasing its joy in the water, I remembered that Bergie, our neighbor, had brought over a fine bunch of garlic, given to him by an Italian at the Asti cafe, and a sack of onions.

Bergie and his wife saved Goldie the Dog from the dog catcher three days ago; I reciprocated with a big zucchini; he brought over the garlic and I'll be taking them a rose.

Crushing garlic into soup water is like winning an unbreakable promise. I cut two onions and cry with contentment. The show was on the road. Onion chunks give a beginning soup the stability of Uncle Harry's suspenders.

Tomatoes in the fridge have been waiting in line from the garden. I threw in 10 or 12 whole or sliced ones. They are like whole and half notes to my peasant symphony.

I have not learned yet to patient it out between stock and soup. I'll chill it to remove the fat, then continue it like a mystery serial.

Using canned stock is not the way, but I confess I give in now and then. It's not the same as falling to the level of using packaged cake mixes (I equate women who use cake mix to those who wear those horrible plastic curlers in public), but until I conquer what Alexander Dumas called the "eternal kettle" filled with cooking leftovers, I will probably weaken to the can and cube.

The hour is late, but I have passed the point of no return. I am trapped, but I am humming. It is Disneyland watching the kettle fill with vegetables.

I do a little dance to the drum beat of the knife striking board through celery and carrots.

Ah, peppers. I toy with an urge to snip in my hot peppers. I am known among the latter-day Escoffier crowd as having a hot mouth, but I must take care or I will soup alone.

My peasant soups are to be wallowed in, not watched en route. For I have my standards.

Barely wash the vegetables.

Never peel. Cut in hardy chunks because it feels so good to the eyes. The pot's innards grow heterogeneously, like a cocktail party.

I throw in five turnips BECAUSE THEY ARE THERE.

What's this? A watermelon rind left on the counter—chop, chop, chop, in it goes.

In go some zucchini and parsley. Help! I can't stop myself.

Over there!

It's my undershirt, dropped on the kitchen floor by someone on the way to the laundry room. I'll just throw—hold it! Maybe it might be a bit much—y'now how finicky are wives and daughters.

Now the mess is simmering gloriously.

Found some radish leaves. In.

Also, a must, a glass of Red Mountain to draw the flavor from the marrow, but please to make sure there's one glass for the cook.

Aaaaaah! Down the hatch.

The soup and I.

We are now one.

~

My wife phoned the office and said the kitchen sink plumbing was leaking and should I call a plumber?

I said, "Who do you think I am, Ted Turner?"

She said, "Can't we play guessing games tonight after dinner? There's water gushing all over the place."

And I said, "Just take it easy, we can't rush to extreme measures over every little crisis."

"It's not a little crisis," she said.

I said, "How do you define a large crisis?"

And she said, "Well, it's the type of a crisis that you'd better do something soon because your grandson can't swim, and I'm only on lesson two in my lifesaving course."

"Please calm yourself," I said. "Tell me exactly what seems to be the situation."

She said, "I can't tell you exactly, because I have a bedspread over the faucet, but I can tell you what it seems like; it seems like the house is sinking!"

She was using her high-pitched voice.

The same voice she used in our old house when the bathtub fell through the floor.

"Don't be ridiculous," I said, waving to a passing female reporter.

"Tell me how not to be ridiculous floating here in front of the phone in my water wings, and I will gladly try."

There was an edge to her voice.

I counseled, "What about calling Bergie the Neighbor? He's the chief fix-it man for the neighborhood."

My wife said, "I did. He's in the living room trying to swim toward the kitchen, but the current's too strong."

I now detected a fleck of emergency in her delivery.

The same intensity as when her brother announced he was voting Republican.

She said, "You have a personal involvement."

I said, "What do you mean?"

"Your golf clubs just floated by."

I perked up.

She added, "I just saved your last score card—180!!!"

I shouted, "YOU HAVE MY BOWLING SCORE!"

And she said, "At DeLaveaga?"

And added frantically, "Will you please make up your mind what action you're going to take?"

"There's no need to get cranky," I said. "Any marriage counselor will tell you that a man and his wife should talk things over thoroughly and then make a decision together."

And added, "So let's start with the premise that a problem exists."

"Hurry," encouraged my wife.

"The faucet is leaking. Right?"

My wife said, "That's what I've been trying to tell you!"

"Now which side of the faucet is defective?"

My wife said, louder than was necessary, "I can't tell you, but the bubbles seem to be coming up on the right side of the kitchen!"

"I see," I saw. "Now we are getting someplace. Do you suspect a worn washer?"

My wife said, not too clearly, "Yesi ible thinkell ubbleoberum bllutummmmmmm!"

I said, "Are you eating something? Please speak more plainly so we can get on with the task before us."

I think she said, "UMMFUL UBBARBLY HELPABBLBILE SIBLE OVERLYM FLABBUBBLE BLUB!"

Becoming a bit piqued, I said, "Listen, dear, calm down. Now let's begin again. Dear? Operator, we seem to have been cut off!"

~

A CLOSET ASTRONAUT

With growing opportunities for citizen astronauts, I wondered recently if I had the stuff to stand being enclosed in a confined space, such as in a space suit or in the shuttle itself.

In the coming years, more earth persons will be spending months in such spaces.

Ergo, to sample how our space personages endure such rigors, I decided to shut myself in our bedroom closet.

In the name of science, I kept notes.

6 p.m.: Said goodbye to wife. She thinks the whole idea is insane. Had to call in six-year-old neighbor boy to shout out a countdown to give the experiment a touch of realism.

6:10 p.m.: Entered closet. While waving before lift off, I closed sliding door on right index finger.

Had boy stop at five and hold, until I could go to the bathroom and get a Band-Aid.

6:15 p.m.: Successful launch. Felt a sense of elation.

6:39 p.m.: Sure is dark in here!

7 p.m.: Called out to wife that I was thirsty. Wife would not bring me a drink. Said I should have thought of it before lift off.

7:20 p.m.: Whistled half a chorus of *Five Foot Two, Eyes of Blue* to combat loneliness.

8 p.m.: Hear door bell. It's the Avrils dropping over.

Wife came to closet door and hissed, "It's the Avrils, you'll have to come out!"

I told her, "I can't. I'm in orbit!"

Her hissing neared hysteria. "I'll say you are! But if you think for one minute I am going out there and tell the Avrils you are in the bedroom closet and won't come out—they'll think you're nuttier than last Christmas' fruitcake!"

8:02 p.m.: I told her, "Well, I'm not giving up my experiment for the Avrils—over."

8:30 p.m.: Hear Avrils leaving, saying they hoped I'd get rid of the flu soon and that it really was unusual to hear of people having flu in August.

I am realizing this is a dumb place to hold this experiment. I forgot to bring a chair.

10 p.m.: Have been standing between my summer suit and bathrobe. To pass the time I went through the pockets. Found a pack of Rolaids, a ticket to a Ming vase exhibit, and the missing key to one of our earth cars.

Midnight: Locked on to automatic pilot and slumped in corner for sleep period.

Calculated that I should be over Decatur by now.

Also observed that isolation can make one feel very isolated.

1 a.m.: Sulked.

2 a.m.: Hear wife thrashing about in bed outside closet and talking in her sleep. I make out "nuttier 'en a fruitcake."

Observed that people with visions are often ridiculed.

8 a.m.: Woke up in a tangle of dresses, hangers, hats, and suits. Strong odor of bacon frying.

Shouted out, accusing wife of holding frying pan next to closet door. Wife confesses.

9 a.m.: Sulking.

10 a.m.: Hungry as a bear. Ate Rolaids. Started hallucinating that neighbor boy was in school discussing my experiment at Show and Tell!

Noon: Avrils come over with hot soup for me.

Mrs. Avril said their six-year-old daughter came home from school with the strangest story she heard during Show and Tell. "What kids won't make up," she said. Never heard my wife laugh so bitterly.

1 p.m.: Decided experiment is a failure. Came out of closet with wife's hat on head where it had fallen from shelf above. Arthur the poodle attacks, biting my leg.

Astronaut material I am not.

But I think I appreciate our astronauts more than the average person.

~

CHAPTER **8**

GRAMMA

GRAMMA AND THE NEWS

After a career writing news and thousands of columns in the United States and as an editor of an *American Service Personnel* paper in England, I approach this chapter with a strong sense of awe.

Did my simple interests during my few summer weeks in my Gramma's environment foretell my future life's profession?

Seemingly she lacked a concern with what was happening elsewhere, while I was a chatterbox.

Thinking back, which takes considerable ergs, I realize that Gramma was never hungry for news the way most people are who are isolated.

When I was in knee britches spending my summers in her woodsy lair, we had neither radio nor newspaper.

Still the sun came up and it went down again.

Which wasn't news.

If the day progressed in a cattywampus fashion, Gramma would have simply decided that the Lord was trying something different and let it go at that.

President Roosevelt launching the New Deal or King Edward VIII abdicating the throne to marry an American divorcee, or "wrong way" Corrigan flying from New York to Dublin seemingly on a whim, would not have excited her had she been breathlessly informed.

In early summer, when my father delivered me via his Maxwell convertible to Gramma's little home in the mountains (to me the coastal range on the lip of the Pacific were mountains and shall continue to be deemed so in order to maintain my musing mood), we would sit on the old bench by the rain barrel to talk and eat wild blackberries on her "rock biscuits" with raw milk.

My father, a city attorney and justice of the peace, would discuss the news while Gramma, always aproned, sat with one hand to her cheek, a gesture denoting flabbergast, which, if translated into words, could become "laws!," "did you ever!" or "merciful heaven!"

I think she just as much savored her son's deep courtroom voice and wordy eloquence in the telling of the happenings beyond her mountain world.

Her responses to blockbuster events were short and repetitive.

All bad news was pretty much accepted as the result of sinning.

Good news rated a "Thank the Lord!"

Very little news was made in her clearing, surrounded by woods.

I remember one time I was on a nearby hill gathering berries and wood, when a gigantic dirigible appeared in the sky over the ridge.

I tore down to the house, yelling, "Gramma! Gramma! Look in the sky!"

She came tottering out, mouth askew, her hands held upward in religious alarm.

She looked up and warbled, "IT'S A SIGN!!!!"

I yelled, "No, Gramma, it's an airship. It's carrying passengers!"

We stood in the clearing, shading our eyes like two lonely earthlings saluting, as the great silver cigar-shaped balloon slid by and over the horizon of forest.

Later, when we were lighting the kerosene lamps for the

evening, we got to snickering over her reaction. She confessed that during her years on the Wyoming plains, she never saw anything fly but birds.

Otherwise the sky was generally reserved for heavenly objects.

The news she liked best came from simple occurrences.

Such as what I saw or did in the woods; how a deer and I stared at each other for a full minute before it moved away slowly; or a complaint that the outhouse needed a sprinkling of lye or ashes.

Probably the best conveyer of happenings was my Uncle Ray, who lived about a mile through the woods and down in a dale.

He would appear at odd times bringing supplies like sweet-smelling apples and fresh picked corn whose kernels would pop juice when pressured by a thumbnail—and we would sit and talk of bloated cows and the price of hay.

Or, of old Mrs. Spanners, a "mile off" neighbor, who was butted into the farm horse trough by her goat ("LAND O GOSHEN!") but who was rescued by Ned Gruts, the traveling blacksmith who happened to be passing and heard her screech.

I never heard two people guffawing like Gramma and Uncle Ray—slapping their knees and carrying on.

Uncle Ray had a high musical laugh that was candy to my ears. It punctuated the telling with him fighting to let the apex of the story through.

During another visit he got Gramma going again telling how the family's living room Victrola started up by itself in the middle of the night, "scaring us half to death playing *Hello central give me no man's land.*"

He said everybody roused up thinking he was in the fermented blackberry juice and was having a party of one.

Gramma would rock with mirth, making Uncle Ray tell it all over again before he left.

Then, about lamp lighting time, my uncle would take his empty milk pail, mess my hair as a parting gesture, and disappear into the dark woods with about a mile to go before he slept.

For two weeks or so we would see no one.

Out beyond the Pacific and over the hills, great, shattering events were upsetting stomachs and shattering nerves.

Not us.

Gramma would play her concertina, click her false teeth to four-four time, and cackle when she thought of Mrs. Spanner and her goat.

It probably wasn't so, but I thought I freshened up her sense of the news. Our get-togethers resulted from some breathless happening in the forest.

Our daily paper was usually an afternoon edition—only there was no paper, no print, no society section.

There were words—usually in lively bursts: "Gramma, I saw a little fawn just a half hour ago!!!"

"GLORY!!!"

That was the headline.

The lead was, "I saw it in the grove below my tree house spread out like a sawhorse wet and wobbly. Its mother was licking it."

It wasn't difficult finding news items in the woods, and it got so she looked forward to my reportorial bursts.

Another day's headline might be, "I saw a giant spider pop out of its ground trapdoor and attack a caterpillar!"

"As I live and breathe!!"

"Gramma, I climbed an oak so high I saw Mexico!"

"GRACIOUS!!! What an imagination!!!"

"The scab on my knee came off!!"

"Lord love you boy!!!"

"I dropped my favorite marble shooter in the outhouse guest hole!!"

"I think we'll just leave it there."

Gramma was editor of our religious page.

Her editorials were earth shaking.

"Jesus is on his way, boy!!"

"Gramma, you said that last week."

This did not phase her one whit.

Nor one iota.

She knew the facts, and out would come her page-worn Bible, and her voice grew bold and strong. "Watch therefore, for ye know neither the day nor the hour when the Son of Man cometh." Matthew 25:13.

And that was that!

~

I can now reflect with a certain amount of poetic nostalgia on my Gramma's mountain outhouse—it being long removed from its malodorous realities.

It was architecturally standard in structure, and, with its half moon cut above the door, artistically correct.

Even though her environment was lacking the modern amenities of her day, she was quite at home with kerosene lamps, hauled up water, wood cooking stove, and the outhouse.

It was as if she had an agreement with nature. They seemed to work together. She seemed pleased with the balance.

The outhouse stood on a hillside in full sun, fringed by a full array of oak and dark green madrone, pine, and crazy-armed manzanita, and tied to her cottage oh, 30 yards away by a path, white with age and sculptured smooth by the repetition of use.

As I said, the building was traditionally shaped and utilitarian as a building can get, unpainted and richly etched by the seasons—but well kept. Except that it was a TWO HOLER!!!

Many a time I sat ensconced trying to visualize Gramma sitting beside me and embarrassingly rejecting the image before it was completely formed.

Yet I supposed it was soberly used as such—like the modern-day guest bathroom, only a bit cozier. I never did dast discuss it with Gramma.

When I was in U.S. Keds, spending melancholy summers with her, one of my chores was to tote buckets of water from the big wooden rain barrel, up to the outhouse and slosh it about thither and yon until the pungent odors of its innards were temporarily quieted.

As outhouses go, it had its charm.

Seated firmly on one of the two holes, one could view, through the open door, a vista tourists drive great distances to behold.

There was a mile of descending forest and, beyond that, the stark cobalt blue of Monterey Bay and the ruled horizontal of green against a blanket of cerulean sky.

An occasional toy freighter set me to dreaming about travel.

Fishing boats speckled the inner bay and sails seem to lay their triangular whiteness against the water.

And in high wind the little Sam Howdy rocked and whistled forlorn songs but never gave in.

Like Gramma's whole world, the outhouse was a place of great quiet, except for the occasional finely honed hum of insects.

One of my pastimes, born of some inner artistic bent, was to collage the interior with Montgomery Ward catalog images—mainly of studiously selected things I desperately wanted. I pasted the interior with these images.

Oh, bright red bicycles, fishing equipment, bar bells, pocket watches—and sophisticated square-jawed, pipe-smoking men modeling the latest suit fashion, and ladies in the latest fashions.

And in a moment of town-learned modesty, I rigged a cleverly hinged sign which I could release from my hole inside which read, "IN USE." Gramma accepted it with gruff humor.

"Lands boy, I reckon both of us never have to go at the same time anyway," she said, with a high cackle.

At night—that was a different kettle of fish. At night the outhouse became a sinister place when approached alone by lamp light.

It threw moving shadows, and the wall of forest just beyond the building was filled with watching eyes (I knew) and the dark hole into which I fitted my bare bottom taunted my imagination something horrible.

I thought of gigantic spiders with blood-red eyes, below licking their fangs to get at my cheeks!!

Years later when I read the *Telltale Heart*, by Edgar Allan Poe, my mind flashed back to the old outhouse.

I had to squelch my feelings about the two holer.

Once, during a terrible stormy night, when the winds flapped the shutters and made moaning noises around the corners of the cottage, Gramma and I leaned into the gale to the old outhouse in the dark.

I was joyful, VERY happy that there was another hole beside mine.

~

GRAMMA'S EARS

Gramma had ears like other people but, when I knew her, sometimes they did not work so well as such.

On the other hand ...

Part of her was frail, but there was spunk when she needed it. She was effective against the rigors of life.

I kept speculating on her age as I struggled with this recollection.

Through her moods and mental frolics my mind felt her older—so whilst writing this piece I am comfortable with the 80s.

She was not deaf, but some incoming words slowed down at her ears. However, at times I give her credit for using this as a defense against incidental prattle.

I'll furnish some examples.

In conversation, when she was interested, she would do just fine.

Out of doors in a brisk breeze she might use both bony hands behind her ears.

This could be risky, however. It tended to blow her out of hearing range.

The summers I spent with her, there were minor mix-ups in communication.

For example: If I came in for supper and exclaimed, "Gramma, it was fun today," she would likely laugh and shake her head as if I was a mixed up young'un and say, "No, boy, it's Tuesday! Monday was yesterday."

"No, Gramma," I said, "I HAD FUN TODAY!"

"Well, I'm glad to hear that," she'd say, refusing to admit that she had heard me wrong the first time. "But you don't have to shout the walls down!"

Another example might be when we played checkers on a lazy afternoon thick with quiet, on a regular board only using black and white beans, with double beans as kings and queens.

I remember once, I had her blocked with a king.

I commented, "Gramma, I think I'm winning."

She consoled, "No you're not, boy, only if you played on Sunday."

In deference to her years, I would go along with these occasional misheard retorts, even when they made trouble for me.

Like I might be out in the outhouse, and she'd call my name "WARLUS" from the cottage.

"What?" I'd answer.

"What?" she'd warble, leaning a cupped ear out the door.

"WHAT???" I'd repeat.

She'd get irritated, "BOY, WILL YOU QUIT ARGUING WITH ME!!!"

She could sit through a Sunday sermon and not miss a word, although once when the preacher asked the congregation to "turn to hymn number seven," she turned to 11 and sang, *Give Me That Old Time Religion* clean through, stomping her foot to her time, while 70 other worshipers sang *Old Rugged Cross*.

I think this was partly due to her fierce pride and, having once started off on the wrong song, she decided to see it through.

Actually, the singing of it had a rather thrilling contrapuntal flavor to it—roughly like *Row, Row, Row Your Boat*.

What made it frustrating was her rebellion against my attempts to compensate by speaking louder.

"Hush your yellin'," she'd snap. "I'm not deaf!"

She was seemingly satisfied with her pick and choose existence, and now I can understand.

If enough people would adopt this attitude, eventually Mother Nature would help us develop ears with shut-off valves so that we could hear only what we wanted to hear.

I think Gramma could control her hearing to a certain extent.

On the evenings I did not want to do supper dishes, I would offer to do them, but almost in a whisper.

"That's very kind of you, boy," she'd say in a flash.

~

My Gramma, who sculpted four children in the harsh plains of Wyoming, knew about the restlessness of weather on kids.

I knew her, of course, when she was almost biblical in age, tall and hard like a girder.

She stood so straight that her dresses fell from her bony shoulders like a flag on a breezeless day.

We looked down on the beginnings of Monterey Bay and northward to the open sea where far off freighters crawled like dark floating insects.

We could see no signs of human life around us or where human life housed itself. There was no Highway I that now cuts below and through the land, between Santa Cruz and Watsonville. Beyond these towns east rises another range and beyond that another and then beyond the San Joaquin Valley towers the mighty Sierra Nevada. That's California for you.

Being isolated the way we were, a summer storm became like a personal visit. We seemed to see them first. Although this is probably not true.

Thunder was its drum corps. It announced its distant intention and Gramma and I hurried out to watch the show wash over us.

We were cut from the same cloth, Gramma and I, when it came to storms.

The drum major in this one was carrying a baton of lightning. As if on some split-second cue, it cleared the way for spits of thunder which clapped and drummed hellishly forming great dark breast-shaped clouds.

In the pre-excitement came a brisk wind, as if heralded by heavenly proclamation. It was becoming a special show, and I am quite pleased that all this stayed with me. Muscular tan oaks waved their spatula like leaves exposing heavy round light gray limbs: a eucalyptus grove bowed ponderously like a corps de ballet in slow motion. Down below us, tips of pine tops waved excitedly like teenaged girls at a rock concert. The spread of distant bay turned a slate gray, fawning before a massive darkening cloud cover.

Gramma and I were meek guests as the storm unleashed this thunderous panorama.

My father, who was a lawyer and judge, was also a fine artist, and Gramma mentioned she had encouraged him to study art, and I am remembering he would find time to walk with storms.

So here we stood, as ugly cloud masses roiled over us and thunder claps rattled our ear drums and rain entered the drama and the rocking bay below resembled a Winslow Homer seascape.

The approaching storm carried with it a hundred tympani playing triple forte.

Fierce gusts of air whipped Gramma's apron around her gaunt body.

There was wildness up there, and then it poured like it had orders to send us inside where we belonged.

She had rigged her little home for the storm.

She fetched down from a curtained shelf an extra kerosene lamp with its sparkling glass chimney.

Extra wood stuffed into the firebox of the Universal cook stove soon had the small kitchen as comfortable as an old yard coat.

The warmth spread into the sitting-bedroom as heavy rain added a cozy drum roll on the roof.

One wall, the one facing the sea, was taken up by a picture window which now featured a glistening waterfall.

The storm affected both of us. Thunder seemed to press us down like a massive rolling pin. In the warmth of the kitchen, our spirits had risen several notches. Gramma decided to bake cookies and corn bread.

Her kitchen smelled sweetly of fresh, raw cow's milk mixed with the musty montage of homemade cheese, drying wild herbs, homemade bread, and wild blackberry pudding in her "refrigerator."

By refrigerator I mean a wire-framed cupboard extending out of doors from the kitchen and covered by burlap material.

And the rain fell and fell.

We could feel, we thought, that the earth welcomed it all.

We saw the thunder and unruly rain as hardy guests.

My Gramma and I seemed a speck, meek hosts of a troubled intruder.

She knew storms. Her memories were of the rolling plains out of Medicine Bow, Wyoming.

She called it a grand stage on which towering cloud cities moved with majestic grace, lightning that roared its accompaniment.

She liked to watch outside, as if wanting to feel a part of our storm, and we would watch the approaching roiling clouds build over the bay.

There was a wildness up there, a magical, magnificent oneness with nature that never left me.

We were frequent visitors to Blackberry Hill that overlooked rolling hills of another distant range.

With the oven hot, it inspired berry cobbler, dribbled with thick cream from Uncle Ray's Guernseys.

And the rain continued and the roof roared back.

I think Gramma cherished the storms, for she would perk up. We would play such unlikely games as Pick-up-Sticks, an old silliness of throwing colored sticks into a pile and, with tweezers and button hooks, take turns caaaarrrefully unpiling them without disturbing others on the pile.

Then she would take up her concertina and sing, *"Bringing in the sheaves. Bringing in the sheaves—we will go rejoicing, bringing in the sheaves."* For many years I never knew, but wondered who Mr. and Mrs. Sheaves were.

The torrent of rain would bring up the Noah's Ark story—rather worrisome the way she told it. All it took was a rain for 40 days and 40 nights, and once I put down the rainy days on paper.

At night, when the house creaked and groaned from the wind, I would think I felt us starting to float.

But, of course, we never did.

~

Old eyes do not waste tears.

Most cry in retrospect.

The memory of my Gramma expressing great sadness is as clear as reflections in a spring pond.

Gramma was tall.

She usually wore a faded calico dress that hung from coathanger shoulders like an unfurled flag.

Minnie—that was her name—never cried conventionally, as I remember, I mean, like I yipped loudly in answer to pain and disappointment.

Her tears seemed born of introspection.

Or perhaps it was a form of penance—for she was an incessant Bible reader, and sometimes she seemed to bend under the responsibilities the words laid on her mind.

But she spread the woe around.

"Boy," she would suddenly sigh, after a long silence, "the Lord is so burdened with this sinning world."

This might be an introduction to something she was reading —like Psalms—"my soul melteth for heaviness—strengthen thou me according unto thy word."

This was not an emotion of any regularity.

The suggestion that Jesus wept no doubt inspired tears of sympathy or agreement, but never of self-pity.

I think at her age she would leak a tear or two for the downtrodden.

The questioning stare of a youngster about to awkwardly offer comfort would induce a sudden assuring smile.

And she would put aside such musings as if to conclude that, of course, I was still free of the disappointments and inevitabilities of oldness.

And so the days representing time unraveled. Her occasional tearing was accepted like morning mists, not understood but quietly accepted.

Understand, Gramma wasn't weepy. Just so you know.

~

I considered myself lucky when I lived with my Gramma during those summers on the mountain.

Very lucky.

I had only to bathe once a week and this was on Saturday night after dark. The occasion was referred to as "tub night."

Saturday was referred to me in this vernacular, as Sunday was "holy day," when she would dwell on the Second Coming or Judgment Day, whilst peering dubiously at me over her spectacles from her high-backed rocker.

While she was technically a grandmother, I remember her not as grandma, or as our daughter tags her grandmother as "grammy," or our two sons "granma." I distinctly remember my down home "Gramma!" which I suppose fit the rugged environment.

Monday at Gramma's was wash day and on Tuesday we picked wild blackberries on a ridge overlooking the verdant fruited plains of Pajaro Valley. Or we made soap and cleaned the lamp chimneys and trimmed the wicks.

The remaining days were mine to roam (but not too far), or chase huge butterflies, or lie silently on my tree house to breathlessly watch various forest residents pick over food I had spread below.

Or join Uncle Ray's wife, Grace, on a day hike a mile or so down to the beach to dig for clams.

The tub night ritual started with heating water on the iron Universal wood stove in large kettles which rocked and spit in complaint of the heat. As it heated, the afternoon waned to just about the hour that the kerosene lamps were lit.

Water came from the well far below and was hauled up the dirt road once a week or so by a laboring Model T truck cut down from a coupe. It made a cheap metallic stuttering call that started faintly and hauntingly and, as it fought the winding climb up to our little house, its engine grew in doubt as its skinny wheels fought the deep ruts for traction.

The water was silvery fresh and burning cold. And always accompanied by several pollywogs which were added to my wilderness Mason jar aquarium.

At my request, a large wooden lard tub was rolled down from behind the outhouse during the day and leaned near the back screen door, ready for its role.

Here I must confess. No way was I going to bring the tub down in the dark. I had experienced, real or imagined, flashing eyes reflecting moonlight in the dark forest. No-sir-ee! This way I was outside and bumping that tub back into the kitchen before you could say Jack Robinson.

It was dark before the water in the big pots on the stove was hot.

The woman who I grew to love was old, but not bent; tall, raw boned, thin, and basic as an old hat. She seemed quite content. She never insisted on having electricity or piped-in water or a bathtub in her little house. At least she never mentioned it when I was with her.

About the only innovation I can associate with her were her false teeth which clicked habitually in the silence of the small living room, like an erratic grandfather clock.

This was the silent time of my life. The forest around us was silent; the air up on the mountain was silent. Gramma spoke softly, often complimenting her good friend with, "Praise the Lord" rather loudish and exuberantly and she would shout "WARLUS" (her version of "Wallace") loudly out the door to "fetch" me from the woods.

When Gramma shouted, her voice mostly came apart—as a sort of yodel.

I visualized it from my tree house as squaw language and would work up the nerve to answer:

"Me come!"

By Saturday evening I had accumulated a marvelous con-glomeration of odors and dirt. It was alleged. Smells that up here one became used to and at home with.

There were certain categories one could consider outstand-ing—oh, such as smoke; skunk, from being surprised too close to one with newborns; an array of odoriferous weeds that usually lingered in the woods where I played. I think by standing next to me one could name trees and pungent weeds and stink weeds of the forest.

And a bit of sweetness from picking wild blackberries.

Plus a fragrant mixture of bay and laurel from the trees I climbed; skunk cabbage and mountain mint and wild honeysuckle from my many hideouts.

There were also the odors from woodsmen and relatives from other hills and dales who came visiting and left their brand of mountain perfume after they had departed.

The Saturday tub bath temporarily released all this from my body and gave me a strange detached, rather sterile sensation, foreign to my summer olfactory presence.

Pulling a wash rag across my stomach would reveal a path of forgotten white skin.

Such cleanliness temporarily set me apart from all that I cherished about my summer life here.

I never remember her mentioning that "cleanliness was next to Godliness." I think now that up in those hills in those times, exceptions were made.

Kids today are detached from odors.

They are disinfected, decontaminated, pasteurized, sanitized, hygenized, purged just to be on the safe side.

Tub night was held in the tiny kitchen in the light of one lamp and the flickering glow from fiery embers in the stove's open fire box.

I found it a rather festive affair in a dim, shadowy, melancholy way, isolated by woods, filled with my imaginations, fears, and accented by the snugness of our tiny cottage.

With the tub water hot and the stove throwing out pleasant heat, the old lady would retire with her Bible to the one other room and ease wearily into her high-backed rocker.

In the dim, yellowish light of the kerosene lamp and the orange-ish flickerings from the open cook stove firebox, I felt a warm, snug joy.

Occasionally she would feel obliged to shout washing instructions.

"DON'T FORGET THE EARS!" as if I had forgotten to bring them into the tub.

"Wash yer feet twice!"

"That neck was awful dirty!"

The rest of my body was left to providence, except for some reason, my belly button.

She merely cackled, "Wash where the horse bit you!!"

It was not until the following year that I learned she meant my belly button. I thought for sure she meant my "pisser," as I called it then.

Gramma made her own soap.

Made it from ashes, lye, tallow and rosin, bugs, and various bits of the forest. It came out yellow and smelled of ashes, lye, and tallow. I was always tracking it down because it always sank.

But it disinfected, decontaminated, pasteurized, and no doubt sanitized!!

It took off anything you wanted to take off—and more.

When I emerged from the tub, toweled, and turned my rump toward the firebox, my Gramma came in with an extra lamp and leered over her bifocals at my ears, and gave a "just-as-I-thought" grunt and drilled in with a wash rag until I thought I felt it emerging through the opposite side!!

For some reason she expected a clean belly button, only she sometimes said "where the chicken hawk bit you."

I stared vacantly the first time until she cackled and furthered explained.

For our Saturday night post-tub frolic, she would make hot chocolate, and from out of nowhere would appear a sugar cookie.

Then we would retire to the small-bed-living room in our nightgowns—me to a straight-back chair, she to her rocker where she would play hymns on the old concertina and knead her lips in strange accompaniment.

In my narrow bed my mind drifted to the well and nest of baby skunks I had discovered near my tree house and the owl performing his mournful serenade, and deeper back into the forest a coyote gave a short recital.

And Gramma whizzed away, *"There is power, power, wonder working power in the blood of the Lamb."*

~

Milk is not the milk of Gramma's day.

The thing with today's milk is you can't even smell it. Hardly.

No doubt a lot of people are alive today because of pasteurization, and all that, but it's been tampered with and added to so much that I'm surprised that it still comes from cows.

My grandmother fed me milk when milk was milk.

That'd be when Herbert Hoover was president and people drove Maxwells, and listened to *Amos 'n Andy*. That's when I spent part of my summers in her mountain lair.

The odor sets heavy in my memory and rises now and then, like the cream in those old hourglass bottles delivered in the cities long ago.

I remember the odor as actually being heavy.

There was a ponderous heft to the body of the smell, and it dominated her tiny kitchen along with oak in the wood box and pickles in brine and a pungent marriage of dried herbs gathered in the woods.

We were an isolated pair, we were, but we had our own milkman.

A loving milkman, a son, who came to us through the woods, a mile down in a small private valley to the north.

He came from her strong, lean body on the plains of Wyoming. It was luck in those days if the doctor's flying buggy and horse could time a blessed event and lend a hand. If such a person was handy in those days.

Uncle Ray, as I say, lived at the end of a long snaking trail that ran through dark groves of oak and eucalyptus and madrone and up and down hills.

Sometimes I walked back with him for an overnight visit. My main excitement came from watching our milk being urged from his several cows in the damp dawn of his small mountain farm.

Those dawns were rich with a dozen other smells that seemed captured and held in his hollow.

The dew brought out the pine scent, the corral manure, honeysuckle, blackberry ripeness, spit bush sap, and the dank forest mulch building over eons.

Uncle Ray's hands, callused and creased from endless farm chores, provided the miracles before my eyes.

He made the bucket between his knees sing with the rhythmic sting of the forced stream of milk.

He was a performer, as well. That was my belief. With his head pressed snugly against the cow's flank, he teased the milk into the flaccid teats and then began a hand dance.

The white streams crossed each other into the bucket.

A cat named Handy sat by Uncle Ray's flank and he would give it a stray squirt. He would bend the teat and shoot a stream past his left arm right into Handy's open mouth.

And I would laugh at this show and thought they should go on vaudeville.

Handy would swallow what it caught, then lick a ring of errant foam around his mouth.

Uncle Ray would laugh that high cackle of his and invite me to hunker down and catch a stream of my own of the rich liquid.

This seemed to content the cows and they would lower their heads to the rich green grass as the day's light disappeared into the forest.

Once a week, sometimes twice, he would carry a bucket of his milk through the woods to Gramma's house and plunk it down on a special kitchen bench.

Raw milk.

Luscious, creamy, bubbly, warm fluid that lined your stomach with new morning energy.

On milk evenings, Gramma would make pancakes. Or she would bury the dipper into the crock and fill my cup with the rich stuff.

It was clean. Uncle Ray had already strained it through a cheesecloth for whatever that accomplished. I never asked.

Oh, how that thick, rich milk went with pancakes, waiting under a blanket of warm homemade blackberry syrup.

Then he would leave us in the darkness, back through the mysterious woods, swinging his old red lantern.

Once in a while Gramma and I would walk the trail to Uncle Ray's to visit the rest of the family

We would sit around the glow of the stove and two lamps, wife Grace and the two kids, Yimmer and Peggy, and catch up on mountain news, oh, such as the fence that was mended that day, or that a new needle was needed for the old crank-up Victrola (Uncle Ray loved J.P. Sousa and sad cowboy songs); or a coyote or mountain lion took one of their chickens; and the new Montgomery Ward catalog; and that it looked like a summer rain was a-brewin'.

All this was before milk was captured in the cities and punished.

And had the moo removed.

~

Gramma lived so far off the beaten track, very few traveling salesmen ever called.

She called them drummers.

When I was wearing Can't Bust 'Em overalls with the crowing roosters on the metal buttons, I saw two and now I realize that it was a solid chapter of Americana.

Some drummers who called were plum lost, but others, resigned to meager transactions, doggedly sought out any form of remote life.

There was a hint of a road to Gramma's chalet, ruts really, that meandered in bewildering indecision up the mountainside from a more traveled dirt road below.

Growing things found the lack of competition among the ruts a good place to set down roots.

Still a true drummer might gamble that a wanting customer might dwell at the old road's end.

It was hacked out by cousins and a son, scattered about the hills of manzanita, chinquapin, buckeye, and sword fern, following a route of least resistance.

So the tracks were seldom used and often became reclaimed by Mother Nature.

Every few weeks a relative would haul up a barrel of glistening fresh water from a meadow well below in the little valley.

The water was screened to remove the pollywogs and skates and moss and various wiggling things that only a college biologist could name.

We drank the rest of it, cold and pure as the earth could manufacture.

But we're dealing here with traveling salesmen.

So I remember only two of them making it to Gramma's little cottage.

We could hear an automobile complain its way up those ruts from the bottom. If one was not expected, the mystery became exciting, and it grew with each approaching turn.

Mostly they were Model Ts converted into display units. Their engines could not keep secrets, announcing each piston stroke.

There were periods of engine idling while the drivers seemed to ponder the wisdom of continuing. But more than likely, both man and car were resting, girding themselves for continued challenges ahead.

I can only remember impressions of those visits. I remember they were special, rare strangers. We would half expect first words to be, "I seem to be lost. Would you be so kind as to tell me how I can find the Charlie Parken place?"

The salesmen, usually florid of face, topped by Stetson hats which would be removed when confronted with the lady of the house and often, as it was warm, there would be the ceremonious toweling of the forehead with a red bandana.

And recognition of the small boy with a pat on the head.

I remember one drummer drove a panel truck with a faded scene of a country storefront painted on the sides. It smartly set the mood.

When he raised a side panel, Gramma and I must have gawked in amazement, for there, before our very eyes, would verily be a country store filled with hanging merchandise.

A board was dropped down for a counter and we were invited to approach.

Like a waitress reeling off the specials of the day, the man talked us through his wares.

We felt flattered by this private show in the woods. There was the latest house clock that required winding only twice a week and, lordy me, you could read the hands and numbers in the dark, he promised.

Gramma later cackled several times over this with, "Why in tarnation would a body want to look at a clock in the dark??"

There were barber clippers that made me wince with remembered pain of pulled hair (we swells back home had one), real barber shears with the hook on one handle for the little finger that barbers used to give nervous little snaps between attacks on one's head; razor strops, lamp chimneys ("laws, boy, engraved, did you see?"), and black stove polish.

Sarsaparilla cough syrup, castor oil, mustard plaster kits (two "ughs" in a row), and Smith Bros. cough drops.

There were silver thimbles, decorated darning eggs, and curling irons.

Then, with an elegant flourish, the drummer opened a velvet-lined case to reveal an array of lockets, pendants—a glitter of baubles. I honestly do not remember Gramma's reaction, but the scene had to widen her eyes.

I had never seen her in anything except a gingham dress that fell straight over a curveless body. In town, at church, she wore nothing that impressed my long-term memory, except for the hat with a bunch of fruit atop, purchased from one of the drummers.

At any rate I do remember a black comb with a spread of imitation jewelry across the top. She bought it from a drummer and wore it for the summers I visited her.

I remember she bought me a fat fountain pen with a lever on the side that I could pull up to suck in ink. Its nib was gold color and there was a piece that allowed me to fasten it to a breast pocket.

Also, for years afterward, I kept a gyroscope top there, which she allowed me to select. I kept it there because it fascinated Gramma so to see it spin in the palm of my hand.

"Lands, boy, will wonders never cease!!"

After money exchanged hands, Gramma would invite the drummer in for cold milk from Uncle Ray's cows and fresh baked cookies in exchange for tidbits of news around the mountain community.

And then the drummer and his traveling store would rattle and bounce down the rut road, the jangling of merchandise fading until swallowed by the silence that dominated our lives.

And all this was good.

~

THE SAGA OF GRAMMA'S PEARLY WHITES

My Gramma's pearly whites played a significant role in my growing up, for it was the first time in my early boyhood that I had ever seen a human being divided, so to speak.

That is, before she slept, it was Gramma in one place and her teeth in another—in a GLASS OF WATER!!

This drama unfolded during one of those summers of 1929 or 1930, if I have my decades straight, with her in the hills above the sea.

I remember it clearly, for it was the first time I saw her remove her dentures and the frightening consequences it entailed. My single bed was in an alcove across from her.

The impression plowed deep. I wondered if old people began dying in sections.

All this was mixed with growing confusion when she placed them on top of her night table one evening and shuffled into the kitchen for a glass of water.

Obviously then, I deduced, she could walk without her teeth.

I watched the pearly whites from the corner of my eye, half expecting them to leap in my direction!

They seem to be—well, let's put it this way—they grinned!!

Menacingly!

Maybe she ordered grinning teeth. Gramma did not grin a great deal herself. She kneaded her lips much of the time in disapproval of the evil world around us.

Still, I deemed them unfriendly.

Her bedtime ritual was classical.

When in her long nightgown and a nightcap bunched over her gray hair, she would fill a glass with water from the kitchen pail, shuffle back to her alcove bed, turn down the lamp to an eerie glow and, sitting on the bed, coach her teeth from her face.

And, in an abrupt closing ceremony, she plopped them into the glass of water.

I could hear the "plop" across the room.

The sound is as distinct in my memory as the yips of coyotes from across the ridge.

Those teeth of my Gramma's (they were hers like a hat or washboard or hair pins were hers) enjoyed a language of their own.

The uppers seemed to communicate with the lowers in a series of sharp clicks, and I remember they would jabber away in her mouth in the stillness of the bedroom-living room even when Gramma was not talking!

I gradually put it together in my mind, that they were scheming some evil deed against me in the dark of the night. Or they would perform when Gramma sat rocking in her chair, playing her concertina.

Or nodding in silent agreement over some grave passage in the book of Revelation.

Gradually I sensed a pattern, a secret clicking code of some kind.

Her forgetfulness played a part in this fascinating theater in which I was the audience.

Sometimes she would remove them, and, when I asked why, she would say, "Just restin' 'em, boy."

Or sometimes the uppers would "rest" on the kitchen window sill and the lowers under her bed pillow. I never fathomed the motive.

Perhaps they didn't get along.

She would misplace them, and she would call out the back door into the woods where I spent much of my time, "Warlus, come 'ere boy, help me track down m' teef!"

It became sort of an afternoon treasure hunt.

I could never bring myself to touch them.

Rather, I would point them out at a distance, and she would snap them back into place and exclaim, "Whew! If it weren't for your sharp eyes, boy, we'd not be eating supper!" which puzzled me.

I have often wondered down through the years what she did when I was not around.

Those teeth took two to manage.

Looking back now, it is difficult to imagine one being frightened silly by a set of false teeth.

Then it kinda became ingrown.

I suppose if this had occurred in the city with its noises, it would have been a distraction, but up here it was mostly silence. And even when my Gramma spoke, her teeth clicked, as if engaged in some kind of weird Morse code, scheming an escape. This also lodged in my mind.

She mentioned that they were rather new, and thus born in the city but ended up in the deep woods. It could be that they were not happy campers.

My jittery imagination was already inflamed, and this added a new dimension.

In the low flickering kerosene lamp, which threw gloomy shadows about the small room, her teeth continued to take on a hideous grimace of unleashed fury.

They seemed to be waiting for darkness.

It was especially unnerving when she inadvertently pointed them toward me.

I know this because I kept nervous track of their every move.

Then one dark morning they turned up missing from their glass of water!

I first learned of the crisis when she shook me awake, shouting, "TEEF! TEEF! MAH TEEF UR LOOF!!!"

In my grogginess what I thought I heard was, "MY TEETH, MY TEETH THEY'RE ON THE LOOSE!!!"

I knew then it had finally happened!!!

The way they had glared at me from her bed stand, I knew they had been scheming through the night!!!!

They had escaped from her night stand and were crouched in my bed.

MY BED!!!!!

In one frantic leap I sprang upward and began to dance around the room so the teeth could not grab my toes! Or more frightening, my bottom!!

I was yelling gibberish and Gramma was holding her head, trying to calm me down.

"MA TEEF AR LOST FOOLISH BOY!!!!!"

Gradually I calmed down and the search began.

We looked everywhere.

Gramma looked older than her years.

Finally she collapsed into her rocking chair.

Then SHOT UP with amazing agility!!!

"PRASS LA LOR," she shouted, holding her behind.

She whirled and grabbed downward and came up with her grinning dentures.

They clacked in her hands like happy puppies reunited with their master.

Then, using both hands, she directed them home.

And an unbelievable expression spread across her face, dissolving into a wide grin.

"It's a miracle, boy," she said, her eyes round with wonder. "I've been bit by my own teeth!!!!!"

~

At Gramma's, my bed was in the sitting-sleeping room next to the tiny kitchen with a single, thin wood wall between, and of a cold misty morning, from within the warm womb of the thick covers, my morning ears could read her movements.

What hugs my memory are her pancake mornings, a double treat of being able to "read" and mentally savor their preparation through the wall and later pour hot honey over the real pancakes.

The heavy morning silence of those hills made any sound sharp.

I could follow the sequence of movements from her brave rising in the darkness of dawn as if they were words in a mountain story.

I already could picture her—tall as a cornstalk, bony, and so thin that her gingham dress hung limp like a morning flag.

I say this was in the fresh 30s, but her style had the flavor of part of the past century.

Minnie Trabing was cheated out of the richest part of her marriage when my grandfather, a former Oregon Trail freighter, ripped his hand wrestling a steer in a box car and died of blood poisoning.

So I would listen to Gramma start her morning.

The slow hiss of her slippers across the kitchen floor was the first sound out of the darkness that reached my cold ears poking out from my warm nest of blankets.

Then the "ping" of the glass chimney being unpronged from the kerosene lamp base and the faint squeak of the unoiled gear bringing up new wick were the next sounds. It was followed directly by a rough scrape of a big Diamond match.

I could hear it flare and the rosy glow of soft light weakly washed into my world as the fire touched the wick.

The familiar hissing of her slippers across the kitchen floor told me she was going into action.

First came the dull clank of circular iron lids being lifted from the top of the Universal cook stove followed by the soft

collapsing of dampish paper, the snapping
I gathered in the forest), and then the dull th
wood fumbled from the wood box beside the

Silence.

Next I could follow the scraping clatter of iron
returned to their holes, and, out of a new silence,
ing buffeted roar of flames reaching up the flue.

Life now had meaning and Gramma's slippers guid
imagination from the stove to the sink.

There her slippers suddenly stopped.

It was as if she had become frozen into some grotesc
form by the bitter cold.

But seconds later she would hiss back into a logica
pattern.

A strong, curt "clank" told me she was using a dipper to
draw water from the kitchen bucket and I could hear it
cascade it into the enamel wash bowl.

My Gramma was a brave woman. I knew what was coming.
I snuggled for warmth.

She washed cold turkey!

The sloshing icy water against her gnarled face pulled un-
natural animal moans from somewhere deep within her
long, lean body.

This was an overture to the wonder of wonders which
would cause me to raise my head from the pillow to acti-
vate the other ear.

I strained to catch the unmistakable clicking of her teeth
being fished out of their overnight aquarium, to be driven
home in her morning mouth with a perfunctory "snap."

My ears sharply "saw" this ceremony.

With her teeth firmly affixed, her shuffling seemed to
quicken.

The sounds were no longer singular, but symphonic.

The new sounds were superimposed against the back-
ground of the crackling fire, the spit of water on the hot
stove top, and the rocking impatience of an aluminum pan
housing our oatmeal mush on hot iron.

uld hear glasses herded from
e of eggs against crockery,
k can lid being wrestled
a week across the valley
om the udder of a son's

of twigs (which
ud of oak fire
stove.

lids being
the grow-

ed my

ue

of a wooden spoon riling the

sterious movements introduced by
aints of the back screen door which
e rumble of firewood tumbling into the
stove and the refilling of the water bucket
old water barrel outside.

the sounds that I knew were approaching the

thick bacon slabs from Uncle Ray's ranch, crackling
ke a distant forest fire—the dissonant ringing of forks,
knives, and spoons being dealt on the table in an orderly
rhythm.

Chairs were scudded across the floor to the table.

This is when she would shout her first words of the morning: "Better be gettin' up boy afore the hogs get the griddle cakes!"

Which I thought rather peculiar because Gramma had no hogs!!

~

I don't know how many people have lost the knack of feeling and watching the power of a sundown ceremony.

When the sun makes its slow announcement of another day's demise, an onlooker has a rare opportunity to become a visual rider on a turning planet.

And watch the sun appear subservient.

Some of my life's good moments have been when locked in a quiet grasp of a fading day, probably by happenstance, followed by curiosity, then by questions.

I would sometimes climb to a rock below Gramma's cottage, when the sky to the west previewed that it was on the cusp of showing off.

And color would take star billing.

My perch was a flat piece of granite that lifted me above the carpet of dull green manzanita, mothered by groves of oak, madrone, and pine of various nationalities.

Then came the Pacific Ocean which at day's end was gradually losing its jewel-like blue to a light lathering of gray.

I would come here for the main event—the sky.

Even on the eve of a clear day I could catch the bald sun make orange eyes on my Gramma's cottage windows.

And then it would flatten on the distant edge of the sea like a punctured beach ball.

During this Herculean move I would half wait for calamity. Instead it would have me marveling at the calm it instilled.

Those sundowns were powerful statements to a young boy's mind.

Sun and planet so close they appear to almost scrape.

Such intimacy of time and space movement and the thrilling reality it instilled of being aboard a planet as it graciously but barely allows the sun to pass downward.

I could never have squashed an ant or snapped a living tree branch at this hour, for it seemed to induce a moratorium of power over anything living.

So fierce was the humbleness of watching the sun and earth set the night.

I made notes, even back then—notes in my mind—and kept them until they now are yellowing.

I remember the comfortable sadness of losing the day, yet knowing that it would appear again as I next awakened fresh and renewed.

I imagine it was the sundown's splotches of color filling the lower sky like an artist's paint rag. It impressed upon me this feeling.

The sun seemed to pause briefly on the edge of the earth, then was smoothly tugged downward by heavenly stage hands with eons of practice.

Now, at 83, imagining back, if I could find myself on that rock again, I would wonder if van Gogh's eyes had thrilled at the same solar performance.

As a kid, I must have lingered for a moment in awe.

And then it was over.

Slowly came the transitional sounds of nightfall.

Like the last few rings of the smithy's anvil down in the valley below, and the bawling cows calling attention to their aching udders.

More intimate were the cozy sounds above—pans being skidded on Gramma's kitchen wood stove, heating the makings of supper.

Soon, in her high shrilly calling voice, she would invite "Warlus" to come off my rocky ledge to supper.

And that would also mean a shuddering wash-up in icy cold water on the wash bench.

Lamp light was lending the large cottage window a sign of warmth, and I would move down from my rock with great fullness.

And far, far away, someone was watching a sunrise.

~

GRAMMA, THE MOUNTAIN BANKER

My Gramma was a mountain banker.

Not the dressed-up, big desk (with mementos), authority paunch kind of banker.

She had her own system. It was neither eccentric nor essentially sound.

As a kid on her lonely mountain top I was impressed enough to remember her banking ways eons later, now as an old man.

Back then, she was as old and independent as I was young and bewildered. She carried her 80-plus years ramrod perpendicular.

There did not seem to be room for other than bone and sinew.

I looked up to her partly because of the clever ways she handled her money.

Just as the sophisticated banker in the city handles money for safe keeping, by spreading it about in financial transactions such as loans, so did Gramma Trabing disperse her meager funds.

She had seven main depositories around the two-room cottage and outdoors, as secure, I thought, as in any city account.

She possessed the imagination of a pirate when hiding her valuables—spiced with a variety of hidey-holes that delighted the young Robinson Crusoe mind of her boarder.

One of my favorites was in one of the hollow upright brass posters of her bed. The four tubes were capped with removable balls. A roll of bills fit snugly in the tubes—at the foot of the bed, as I recall.

Gramma acknowledged it would be the first place robbers would check after tying us up. The Western pulp novels of her day often mentioned bed posts as a money hiding place.

But she liked the cash handy, and anyway she was convinced she could talk the blighters away from the bed tubes by telling them that's where she kept her dirty laundry!!

My favorite: A portion of bills and an assortment of trinkets rested worry-free in a Mason jar at the bottom of the rain barrel outside under the eaves. The baubles and a few rocks kept the jar submerged like a Jules Verne submarine.

I do not recall one incident where her money might have been threatened. Only relatives or lost hikers ever set foot on the little clearing.

When my father deposited me at Gramma's, he would leave her $100 in $5s, $10s, and $20s. She would pin them together with a note on which she wrote "Charlie" followed by "SPENT!" Not so. The exclamation mark was to inform any bounder that he was out of luck.

As I wrote, those who wrote the Western pulps of the day were stereotyped in their stories when it came to their characters' hiding money.

The ranchers and miners always tucked their savings in mattresses, cookie jars, Bibles, or sewed into hems of skirts.

Passing bandits knew exactly where to look.

Gramma had read those pulps and she was smart. She never put her money in any of those places.

Of course, in my fantasies this meant that we would be tortured when the frustrated bandits could not find the loot.

I used to tell Gramma, when we'd talk by the oil lamp of a night, that I would NEVER give in, but she would say, "Boy, the idea is to trick 'em. The money I buried by the oak with the swing will give 'em what they expect. We'll tell 'em about that one."

I knew about THAT one. She told me of some of her other hiding places, and I felt very honored.

One was 12 steps due west from my oak tree swing where Gramma had buried a small can that had once held Rhubarb Compound tablets for indigestion. The can was inside a larger Folger's coffee can. Each year she would change the outside can to keep her "money" from being eaten by the worms. This was to be revealed if her life was threatened.

By "money" I mean she had wrapped a dollar bill around paper cut to size and made into a roll. She figured it would fool someone in a hurry. Gramma wasn't born yesterday.

As far as I was concerned, this was buried treasure. There were times, I now confess, that I dug it up while playing pirate, but always reburied the treasure untouched.

There was another money cache in the butter churn sitting casually on the open back stoop.

When we needed money for a trip to town, and $4 for church, we would use resources in this hidey-hole.

Her income came mainly from her loyal sons. And the money was pretty much divided in her various "banks."

One which I knew about, but never actually saw, was in the bore of her single-barrel 410 gauge, breech-loading shotgun.

It was kept in a closet.

She occasionally cackled, when we dwelt on the subject, "Wouldn't it be a caution, boy, to hold a ne'er-do-well at bay with this bank?"

"Hell's bells and panther tracks," she'd shout, slapping a thigh with her bony hand. "All I'd shoot would be money!"

There were two other rather clever savings institutions.

One was in the back pocket of a pair of overalls which dressed her garden scarecrow.

Who would ever look in a scarecrow's pocket?

I'll bet it was the smallest bank in the United States.

I would nominate Gramma as the smartest banker anywhere you'd want to name.

Helping to clean, I would come across $5 behind the framed print of Jesus on the cross, and a few inside the works of her eight-day clock on a mantle.

I'd find paper money clipped to the back of curtains. A minor earthquake would have produced a rain of cash from places she had long forgotten.

I found some in a book. I remember because she gave it to me to take home—*Only An Irish Boy* by Horatio Alger.

At home I opened it to read and found $5.

Mending was one of the special occasions involving Gramma and me, because it called for serious teamwork.

Take a lad who had never threaded a needle and an old lady whose eyesight would make a mole's the envy of an eagle in comparison, and you had a team that once attached a button to a shirt tail and had a terrible time trying to find its buttonhole.

We laughed the laughs of jolly bumblers.

Gramma's sewing basket was wicker and brown with a red tassel on the top—a rather dull affair to a kid—but when she removed the top, it released a burst of color from a nest of threads that dazzled me, like my own treasure, a bag of varicolored marbles.

Within the basket, in a tin box with a faded painting of a Wyoming prairie on the lid, she kept her needles and thimbles and a community of buttons large and small.

Also in her basket was a fat tomato-red pin cushion that she said she used when she was raising her "young-uns'" on the windy rolling plains of Wyoming.

Threading a needle was the main event of a mending project.

From her big window we looked down the "mountain" over a roof of oaks that gathered like mounds of green cauliflower to floating diamonds of sprinkled sunlight on Monterey Bay and its big brother, the Pacific Ocean.

But back to Gramma.

She held the needle up, like a posing Isadora Duncan.

Were I rich, I would have paid to have it duplicated in marble.

Rodin style.

At this apex, she pushed the thread end forward as I stood behind her shoulder like a National League umpire, guiding the thread end by voice.

"Tiny bit up, Gramma. Bit to the left—no, right—."

"TARNATION, BOY!!!!! MAKE UP YOUR MIND!!!"

We would surge toward the eye, miss, then retreat and surge again.

I can still see her smacking her lips over the thread end to render it stiff as it hit the needle and frayed.

When she would bunch her bony fingers around the tiny thread, she moved by rote, from years of past mending with sharper eyes.

Gramma would try one eye, then the other, then explode, "TARNATION, BOY, AREN'T WE A PAIR THOUGH?!!"

Then she would laugh again in that high cackle.

"HEEHEEHEEHEEHEEHEE!!!"

"That hole's narrower than a sinner's gate to heaven!"

Finally she would shout, "HALLELUJAH!" when at last the thread end would slip through the needle's eye.

This was always celebrated with, "Praise the Lord!"

I remember it upsetting me slightly. After all my concentration in guiding that thread end through the eye, she gave the Lord the credit.

I didn't dast complain.

Gramma, I suspect, was color blind.

She was not particular in selecting a color.

Consequently, by summer's end my socks had splotches of colors on heel and toe.

Among the more daring experiences in my past was the repair of holes in the seat of my pants, with me in them. I'd rip them climbing trees.

Often she would keep a needle threaded for such occasions.

"I'll be careful, boy," she would say.

And she was, never sticking me, but twice. I would discover getting ready for bed that she had sewn my pants to my undershorts.

"Hey Gramma, look what you did!"

That would put her in a jolly mood.

"Tarnation, boy, stop complaining. You got two mends for one!"

Finally it is impossible for me to forget Gramma in her most amazing display of youthfulness.

I mean for a woman in her 80s.

Because of my MO climbing trees and sliding down rocks, my duds were often torn asunder.

I didn't mind, but the lady of the cottage felt motivated to mend, probably after sewing for four children in the outback.

She could spot a tear in a flash. One time this became a hoot.

When I came in the cottage she was sewing but laid her project in the rocker. I probably distracted her, for when she returned and sat down, she shot upward with the elasticity of a Jack-In-The-Box.

She had either sat on her needle or was training for the Olympic high jump!!!

~

Probably the most tranquil segments of my early life were spent during the peaceful childhood summers with my Gramma.

Oh—except for the violence.

Murder! To be exact!

And I was an accessory after the fact (a person (ME) who assists another (GRAMMA) who has committed a detachment).

To wit: dismembering the head of a stewing hen from its body.

A shuddering segment in a little kid's short existence!

I have to think that God was watching! And approved!

A bit of irony here is that this act of violence was in a setting of blessed tranquility.

In the early 30s, there was a seemingly continuous flow of forests around us. A feeling of exciting isolation dominated one's life.

One's eyes could still rest in any direction and come up with distance. There was still an array of wildlife.

A salt lick up above the outhouse drew deer and wild cats and other creatures from the dark woods in wild cat tense, hesitant segments of movements.

Badger, possum, and fox came in turn for food, in exchange for the pleasure an old woman and a skinny kid got from watching their wary habits.

Chicken hawks soared—heads moving from immobile floating bodies.

We were two benevolent saints. St. Francis of Assisi would have smiled approvingly.

But, as for chickens—WHACK!!

Gramma (now we're getting down to the way it was) read the Bible almost daily, and, if I was within earshot of her summons, which cut through the woods like a mission bell, I would be expected to come "listen to God."

Among the Bible material covered, as she rocked in her spindle-legged rocker, were the Commandments, one of which was, "Thou shalt not kill."

Apparently this did not cover stewing hens.

WHACK!!

She kept a small high wire enclosure pen of them behind the outhouse.

They were replenished now and again by Uncle Ray who lived the other sides of the huge eucalyptus grove, over a couple of hills and down in a small valley.

There was no rooster, though.

Roosters had a natural bent of breaking the dawn and Gramma didn't care to have her dawns bent.

Their sleep-ripping cadences were not "Indian Love Calls," as Gramma put it.

Her small flock produced brown-speckled eggs that freshened our morning breakfasts, along with mush speckled with wild blackberries and raw milk, still warm from the udders, that Uncle Ray brought through the woods. To be perfectly clear, Uncle Ray did NOT bring the udders!

I'll allow she cooked hearty and healthy; however, her mush, bless her soul, could have caulked canoes.

But it kept me standing up straight 'til midday.

It had character.

Surviving it gave one confidence that one could handle ANYTHING!

Gramma's hens did their laying, whether or not they suspected their demise.

Sort of on the Scheherazade principle.

That is, entertain us with eggs or OFF WITH THEIR HEADS!

When she wanted chicken for the table, she would walk up to the flock, like a bony executioner, and point out the victim.

The event would take place the next morning, following a restless night of my fighting dreams of sneaking out into the night and setting the victim free.

I hated it.

My Gramma was, as I've said, a tall mountain woman, who I can't imagine having been born in New York. Which she was.

But much of her young adulthood was weaned on the rigors of the outback of Medicine Bow, Wyoming.

She had shot attacking wolves chasing her winter horse-drawn sled when hauling food to distant cowhands in deep winter snows. Her own uncle died in a blizzard. She had made jerky and ridden a bucking horse.

Even in her 80s, her mind and body were as tough and gnarled as a Sierra redwood.

But, enough of this literary diddling.

On the morning of the execution, I would be dispatched to fetch the hen amid a storm of wild clucking, dust, and flying feathers.

Which I did reluctantly, emerging with the bird in question, my shoes caked with chicken poo—its last will and testimony!

Gramma would be waiting by the kindling stump, ax in hand, her faded calico dress protected by her ever-present apron—standing there like some female Philistine Goliath etched against the distant blue bay.

As I remember, the lethal act could have been carried out in a thrice, except that, as the holder, it was difficult to place the hen's head on the block with my eyes closed, and my head swiveled 180 degrees to the rear.

I managed finally, and the Lizzy Borden of the chicken world wasted no time.

Whack!!

The separated head looked up from the dirt with disinterested eyes as the body flew into its dance of death.

On several occasions it landed on its feet and, with extraordinary navigation, chased Gramma around the stump with malice aforethought.

I thought it quite entertaining, but she monologued, "Stop it, boy!! It's GAINING!!"

When Gramma became excited she yodeled her dismay, like I later compared to Mrs. Franklin Roosevelt, and her high-buttoned shoes strutted ahead of her body, like a vaudeville dancer leaving the stage to music, buck and wing style!

Finally the headless hen lost its will to live and lay still.

A pail of hot water would be waiting by the outdoor wash bench and after a couple of dips, the bird would relax its feathers.

One of the fascinating sights of chicken innards, to me, were the unlaid eggs, white like giant pearls and round.

These would be left on the forest's edge for our forest friends, usually a wild cat or rare mountain lion or coyote.

The sacrificed hen, rubbed with mountain herbs, would take its place in the big iron stew pot in a nest of fresh vegetables and often with lard from a rabbit that Uncle Ray had shot and brought over with the milk.

And then we would thank the Lord, play tug-a-war with the bone, and, if I won, I would wish that Gramma would take that one Commandment more literally!

~

I never knew of my Gramma driving an automobile, nor did she take well to riding in one.

During my time with her she only gave in with great reluctance, and with what she considered as foolhardy adventurism.

All rides were out of the hills to the village of Watsonville.

At the price of having my ears scrubbed, I got to go along on these adventures.

Gramma looked nice and, let's see, what I am clear about is that she wore her round hat with a bunch of cherries on the front. We met Uncle Ray down at the well, so Gramma wouldn't have the cherries bounce off her hat on the devil-may-care ride from her cottage.

She boarded the "T" under pre-agreed-upon conditions:

1. "How fast do you figure on going?" Thing is, back then, how fast was fast? Ray said it depended on how soon she wanted to reach Watsonville! To make sure he had no need to race to reach town (all of 5 miles) before stores closed, we arose at 6 a.m. We staggered down the hill to the well before Uncle Ray was finished milking his cows, and I would trip four or five times trying to walk in my sleep.

2. "Are the wheels on good and tight?" This was her way of kicking the tires.

3. "The young-un and I will sit in the back." She maneuvered into the seat directly behind her son where she could tap him on the shoulder with her cane when she began to panic—which, it turned out, was every quarter mile.

Once in her excitement she used the crook of her cane to pull back on his Adam's Apple, in the manner of one reining in horses.

Those jaunts to town were symphonies of raw nerves, with the "T" rhythmically leaping ahead in uncertain surges, and with Gramma saucer-eyed, shouting "Praise the Lord!" above the tinny clatter.

If my uncle removed a hand from the steering wheel to call our attention to some point of interest, Gramma would whack him on the noggin with her cane shouting, "RAY, MIND THE HORSES!"

In town, she couldn't wait to take to her feet again, her cherried hat askew, and mumbling wildly.

As she stepped down, the "T" backfired as the motor quit, giving my Gramma an extra jolt. She reacted as if some stranger had pinched her bottom!

Watsonville meant three attractions to me.

It meant a store that, if one could imagine, dealt only with ice cream—must have been 100 different flavors. Its clientele consisted mostly of kids standing around licking.

I think I got away with four cones without throwing up!

Second were the evil men lurking in dark bars.

There seemed to be more of these "evil dens" than there were ice cream parlors.

I was very curious to see some of these wild, evil specimens but Gramma prodded me in the back with her cane whenever I slowed down to peer inside the darkened bars.

Thirdly, Gramma told me about the one-armed trombone player who was minister to her church.

On another occasion we attended a service there and, lo and behold, Gramma was right, there he was.

He was a miracle man to my way of thinking.

The preacher would tuck his horn between his cocked head and a hunched shoulder and do a tromboneze of *Give Me That Old Time Religion.*

I swear, the Reverend could make that horn yodel like I would, years later, hear Glenn Miller and Tommy Dorsey do—and they had TWO arms!

My musical hero worship paid off. A tiny group of members who somewhat played musical instruments including Gramma with a tambourine, marched to whiskey row, gathered in front of a bar and burst into a chorus of guilt tunes geared to give the devil the shakes.

I was assigned a base drum which I whacked with enough vigor to surely make the evil drinks dance guiltily on the bars!

A few woozy denizens were lured out.

I think their foggy brains mesmerized into expecting a bevy of dance dollies hired to perform a few buck-and-wings to increase their thirst.

When we collected enough to handle, we lured them, Pied Piper style, and marched them to the church where coffee, sandwiches, sweets, and an earnest sermon were served. I was impressed. Then out they tottered into the night.

Did the one-armed trombone player reach them?

Only after the roll is called up yonder will we know.

~

GRAMMA THE INVENTOR

Yes she was.

Gramma Minnie Trabing invented because she lived alone on a lonely hill top and sometimes had no alternative.

She was old, and invented to while away that oldness.

Some of her contraptions were a little boy's delight.

Later, I thought she should have starred in *Popular Mechanics*.

The mechanical scarecrow was one.

It stood like a military hobo between the cottage and the outhouse and amidst the vegetable rows, stiff and ragged in an old black coat on cross sticks and a battered felt hat. Its arms seemed to beckon rather than scare intruding birds.

Back in the woods, there was no need for pants, she said.

Should a rabbit or bird or deer or raccoon wander too close and Gramma spotted them, she would sneak her hand out the back screen door and give a hanging horseshoe a yank.

Suddenly the scarecrow's arms would fly into the air, with a string of clattering tin cans affixed to the wrists!

And just as suddenly the garden became an exploding zoo.

Rabbits became cross-eyed with fright, birds left floating feathers in their frantic flight, and deer broke high jump records from a standing leap—and, finding traction, disappeared into the dark forest.

For night critters she would make the scarecrow dance in the dark just before we went to bed. It worked fairly well.

That's my report on that!

Another thing, Gramma was forever misplacing things.

Her kitchen pot holder was one of them.

With a hot pan on the wood stove, you can't go fussing about for a pot holder.

Very, very cleverly, one afternoon she sewed a length of ribbon and her pot holder to her apron, just about where it would be handy when she needed to withdraw a hot pan of corn bread from her Universal wood stove oven.

The problem was rightly solved and she never thought to brag of it.

Gramma sewed everything—a habit of necessity while rearing three boys and a girl on an isolated sheep and cattle ranch on the rolling plains of Wyoming out of Medicine Bow, but now, as she would sigh, "My eyes are gone down the road."

In her ancient age, her eyesight was watery, and threading a needle was a frustrating chore. I've already written a piece on our needle traumas.

But what I forgot in that chapter was her clever attempt to get the job done without me or whomever.

She would select a thread color she wanted. Then she would mix a bit of flour and water and goop it on an index finger and thumb.

She let it dry a bit, then pasted the new thread to the short length of the one already threaded in the needle.

Then she would set this aside to dry. When it did she would trim the paste, and pull the new thread c-a-r-e-f-u-l-l-y through the eye of the needle.

The gray-haired old woman had smarts.

My favorite of her inventions was one of a kind.

It was the product of an independent mind, uncluttered with the claptrap thinking of those yammering city folk.

Gramma invented what she called a mouse discourager.

In the forest, mice considered Gramma's place a kind of play house.

They would gnaw tiny holes through the single walls and poke about in the night.

So what she did was to push bits of cheese, wheat, bread, lettuce scraps, and general leftovers through the holes on the theory that the mice would become too fat to fit the holes into the house.

It worked most of the time.

When it didn't, what she had were bigger holes and rounder mice.

Now one wild thing that made me shudder was the ugliest thing on the mountains which we called a wood spider. UGRRRIIEEEE!!!

It favored, it seemed, building its wide web across trails.

Sometimes they were difficult to spot, and both Gramma and I had walked into their webs.

Their eyes seemed yellow and sort of Boris Karloff looking.

So the mountain inventor invented a solution.

She got Uncle Ray to give her an old hat with a wide brim.

Then she affixed a sawed broomstick to the inside middle and, of an early evening or foggy morn, Gramma would march along a trail, slightly holding this contraption before her like a dehorsed Joan of Arc, and sometimes singing *Marching To Zion*!

I clogged along behind, shouting encouragements: "I THINK YOU GOT 'EM GRAMMA!!!!!!"

I could not vouch for them, but I could imagine they were mad as hell!!!

~

There have been few periods or places in my life where I have experienced the total quietness which permeated my Gramma's mountain home.

The kind of stillness that fills the ears with their own ringing.

I can think of moments deep in the bowels of the Carlsbad Cavern under New Mexico. Or along the Muir Trail high on the ridge of the Sierra beside Ray Lakes and Sixty Lakes Basin.

Or once deep in the nave of Chartres Cathedral near Paris.

When I was in U.S. Keds, heck, noise was fun. It felt good to make it; yelling was growth.

But at Gramma's we were isolated from most sounds.

How quiet did it seem?

Well, hold yer hat!!

Now, I find myself daydreaming the memory of them, like ...

When my Gramma read her Bible of an afternoon in her rocking chair, I could hear the holy words enter her mind.

I could hear the sunlight slant into the room and crash yellow against the wall tapestry of a Grecian lady with an amphora on her shoulder.

I could hear dust avalanching down the shaft of light, its great boulders booming like a brace of tympani against an inner wall!

I could hear a web screeching from the body of a spider crocheting a food trap in one high corner.

Back in the woods that almost surrounded the small cottage was my tree platform in the muscled arms of a Live Oak.

Its blotched gray limbs held it high and safe.

I could stretch out, stomach to floor, and watch distant fishing trawlers move silently on blue glass at the mouth of Monterey Bay.

I saw tiny white sails ease by like old-fashioned musical notes as on a silent screen without the piano player.

Sans a breeze, the forest froze in silence.

I would hear the hum in my ear and chastised my brain for making the racket.

I tried to silence even this by freezing my thoughts.

Recently, I read that people often panic when lost in the woods because of their fear of the silence.

I can understand this. It is so rare in our lives. When silence does occur during a 24-hour period, we are usually sleeping through it.

Sometimes it gave me a start. The distant whack of a screen door would break the air like gun shot, as Gramma emerged to throw out a pan of dishwater.

Or sometimes her false teeth clicked.

They broke the silence like castanets out of control!

I would hear other "quiet" sounds from my tree house.

Deer hooves snapping the forest floor.

Badgers and possums brushing against thickets and black wild bees droning into the stillness like loaded bombers.

My father's mother spent family-raising time in the great silent prairies of Wyoming where little was said and less heard.

I think she carried this into her aging, moving her old bones about the house like a vision, awaiting evaporation.

Sometimes in the evening her concertina wheezed mountain harmonies sprinkled with hymns sent heavenward by her creaky-door voice.

On rare occasions I think it provoked a coyote to answer from the edge of the woods—believing it was being courted.

NOW HEAR THIS! I don't suppose the reader is going to become all a-twitter. You're not going to believe that a coyote is going to get all hornswoggled over an ancient lady playing *Rock of Ages* on an equally ancient concertina. But, as I write, this vision popped forth, and I give myself the writer's benefit of the doubt that this tidbit has been in residence, lo these many years, in a cubby hole that deals with reconnecting long lost coyote lore.

So I hope this helps!

Also, when talk built up in Gramma, she would give me guidance, preparing me for when the roll is called up yonder.

Sometimes, there was this thick stillness.

It contented my Gramma.

She used to say, during our walks in the woods, "Let's sit, boy, and listen. Maybe we won't hear anything."

I paid little attention to her oldness.

As far as I was concerned, she was born old.

She seemed to live on, never becoming older than old, as I changed. I did not see her through high school and college, and, while I was away serving in World War II, Gramma passed away.

She did write me a letter saying she was praying for me, and it worked.

And over the years I wrote to her, on and off. So I remember plenty of odds and ends.

She was about as great a human that I could imagine. This probably should have been my opening sentence.

I knew very little about her past. But the fine human being that was my father placed Gramma on a very high plane.

I feel certain that whatever is her address now, she has acquired big time seniority.

I wouldn't mind a letter.

Thinking back, she never spoke of her ancientness.

When we walked a fair piece with hills involved, she would sometimes stifle my pace with something like, "Land sakes, boy, you have legs of a centipede—slow down!"

She might explain this order with, "My bones are savin' for the trip back!!"

Gramma would be of little worth, if following her in order to find shade. She was so stringy and tall, shadows hardly bothered with her.

Gramma had a stock vocal routine when I disobeyed, and it made her feisty. "I can still whup wildcats, boy!!"

The so-called punishment: I would have to go down the rutty road to the willow patch near the water well to "fetch a whip"! I think I would acquire points for saving her steps.

She would take the whip (I would cut the slimmest branches I could find) and put it in the kitchen wood box where it would be handy next time.

We would accumulate two or three whips during my stay.

They would be burned unused.

There was a wonderful casualness in our daily routines. I can still see her sitting on the front stoop playing her concertina of an early evening.

The woods that encased three sides would darken early, and the evening supper fire smoke curled lazily from the chimney.

I might typically be curling chicken wire around the carrot patch to ward off the varmints and deer. And Gramma would be reminding God, "When the roll is called up yonder I'll be there!"

There's not a whisk of a doubt that she made it.

It would be very nice if her concertina was included.